NO MORE BAND-AIDS

Heal Without Identity

CORISSA HOWARD

No More Band-Aids

Copyright © *Corissa Howard*, 2024

All Rights Reserved

This book is subject to the condition that no part of this book is to be reproduced, transmitted in any form or means, electronic or mechanical, stored in a retrieval system, photocopied, recorded, scanned, or otherwise. Any of these actions require the proper written permission of the author.

Table of Contents

Dedication i

Acknowledgments ii

About the Author iii

Introduction iv

Chapter One Identity 1

Chapter Two For me, not against me 36

Chapter Three Training 77

Chapter Four Redemption 121

Chapter Five Grace 143

Dedication

I dedicate this book to my two grown children, Moriah and Chandler. I hope this book will help them remember to share Jesus even when life is not perfect. They witnessed a lot of my maturing in Christ. God used my journey to make them into the spiritually strong adults they are today.

Acknowledgments

I want to thank my husband, Bobby Howard II. He is the reason I am strong and have had the opportunity to homeschool and write this book. He believed in me and sacrificed his own desires for me to fulfill my calling.

I also want to thank my family and friends, especially Carolee Hannah, for not giving up on me. Everyone was very patient and helpful in writing my first book. I hope to have more inspirational moments for writing in the future!

Thank you to Amazon Hub for their professional editing and patience!

About the Author

Corissa Howard is a mother of two, wife of over 27 years, and owner of C5 Fitness, LLC (#C5Life). She enjoys learning as a lifestyle and is currently a nursing student in Georgia. She homeschooled her children from Kindergarten through High School and was a homeschool educator in several programs.

Corissa believes in authenticity, miracles, and mysteries, and she desires to fulfil God's calling through obedience. Her background is in fitness, education, and non-denominational Christian studies. She believes life is full of connected mysteries and encourages people to be comfortable in the discovery of them. Everyone has a story that is unraveling the great and mysterious creator of the universe. Her faith in Jesus has encouraged her to overcome life's challenges entangled with doubt, fear, and worry that good enough is genuinely good enough. Often, we believe life is keeping us in a victim statehood like an orphan child, but when we begin to elevate our perspectives, we then become like a butterfly full of vibrant color, enjoying the beautiful surroundings without a care in the world. Our mental peace may take time and practice, but eventually, it will be present within us.

Corissa encourages you to trust the promptings of the Holy Spirit; though you may not fully understand and even resist, but your surrender will open the heavens to all the love and forgiveness your soul longs to receive. *No More Band-Aids* is about letting go of the label to become someone and just knowing that in Christ, you are all you ever needed to become.

Introduction

Programmed or Free? From 1976 to public school to twenty-seven years of marriage, I was programmed to label! I labeled myself, tried on figurative Band-Aids for identity, and then finally surrendered to the truth so I could live limitlessly without a label. We do not have to be patterned by culture or statistics. People are unique, complex creations that only God can know. Is religion a façade, like a band-aid or a cover-up for what it really is? Which metaphors describe your life? Broadway show, heartbeat, butterfly, Band-aid? Life as a Broadway show is still veiled, used as entertainment. What lies behind the curtain is the real deal! Life as a heartbeat has rhythms of highs and lows. Life as a butterfly has a cocoon stage and then flies in freedom. Life with Band-aids will only limit you to yourself because it's all in your head. You may be controlled by fear, anger, and other limitations. Jim Kwik stated, "If you fight for your limitations, you get to keep them." Are we victims of what has happened to us? Or do we embrace the pain of exposure as part of the plan to the road of redemption? How does one live by grace, love, and forgiveness in a world of plastic Band-aids, almost like mysteries? No More Band-Aids is about how to heal without identity or attachments to the known. If I wanted to stay a victim of my pain story, I would keep repeating the pain story as my identity and hide like a recluse spider living in the darkness, never healing the inner man. My pity never freed me. I believe to live is to die to your selfishness, your past, and your future. We can either repeat being a victim or embrace grace and overcome the pain story. The best solution to my problem came from a friend's question, "How long are you going to stay there?" Think about it!

In 1996, at a church Heart to Heart ladies retreat, I felt the Lord tell me that I would write a book about Band-aids. I thought, *'that's the craziest thing I've heard!'* Scripture states in 1 Peter 3:15, "But in your hearts revere Christ as Lord. Always be prepared to give an answer to everyone who asks you to give the reason for the hope that you have." In 1996, as a new believer in Christ, I was ready to give an answer for the hope I received, but first, I had to go through the fire and learn to let go of my ego. My life is full of miracles and events lining up "for" me, but I was too busy trying to become someone who I thought mattered. I had attachment issues and band-aids in search of love, joy, and inner peace. Ignorantly, I was creating my own prison, believing I was on the path to salvation, yet I was living without joy in many areas I could have left great influence had I heeded the promptings of the Holy Spirit.

This book is a partial glimpse into my life and some mystical connections that helped me to trust the Lord and find inner peace. You will see the hand of God throughout this story and how the shift of my perspective created freedom in my mind to be who I am. I challenge you to consider living by faith, risk your identity in all areas, and let go of emotions that no longer serve your greatest good. You cannot heal what you don't reveal. Emotions may get trapped inside us! I hope this crazy life of mine will encourage you to trust the unknown or the other side of having it all together or being perfect in others' eyes. God covers all our inadequacies and failures with His love, forgiveness, grace, and mercy! Thank God His grace was sufficient for me.

Chapter One

Identity

"All discomfort comes from suppressing your true identity."

-Bryant H. McGill

I call myself a Christian; therefore, some would judge me and put this book in the trash! This book is not just another book on Identity or a religious Jesus book. If you want to know how a "Nobody" is Chosen, keep reading. Many Christians are labeled as judgmental hypocrites; even I have labeled them. A Christian identity holds such a high standard, and I don't know many perfect Christians. Judging others is one of the worst things to do because it divides people. A Pharisee was always looking down on others, thinking more highly of himself. I was like a religious Pharisee with a hard heart, and I felt I could not trust anyone. We may present ourselves as Christians with fruits like kindness and generosity, but underneath, we could be like wolves in sheep's clothing. Our identity is often in disguise until we rise and take our seat with The Highest. We may be denying Christ and not know that our hearts are far from him. You may think, 'Not me!' like Peter, a disciple of Christ.

Sometimes, I blamed others for my limitations, which I had the power to change, but I didn't because the circumstances made me feel guilty. I held onto my pain story, and I trapped myself. I guess you could say I had a '70s Kellogg's problem. I could not 'L'eggo my eggo.' Why do we treasure our significant special circumstances and hold onto our pain story? We think our story is somehow significant to the trap in which we are stuck living in. The truth was, I judged myself. And then, I projected this hurt onto others. My stepfather would say, 'Be careful who you judge (pointing the finger) because you have three pointing back at you." I judged Bobby's Christian younger sister as having it all together. It is an error to judge; we must never judge a book by its cover. When we judge, we make ourselves a little lower or higher, and God has created us all equal. It was like the three fingers pointing back at me were making my heart harder. We are only hurting the world when we hold judgment or anything opposite of love, whether toward ourselves or towards others in the way we label. Often, the ones we judge or the ones who offend us the most are the very ones who help us overcome our greatest struggles. Don't we all suffer? I would shame myself or feel guilty for making a decision that was not well thought out and may have cost a lot of money or wasted a lot of time. I imagined myself as the worst sinner who should feel shame, guilt, and punishment for my sins. I was dying within and did not value what could set me free. I thought I wanted freedom from my circumstances, but God wouldn't let me escape! Shame has no place, but it most definitely had a stronghold for much of my life because I was mentally attached to shame, and that is a heavy yoke to carry! My internal warfare was a battle of who I say I am. As a Christian in a fallen world, trying to get myself in alignment while loving God with all my heart almost drove me to insanity.

In the book of Romans, God turned the people over to depraved minds because they worshipped false idols. I would go further to say that the idol was the identity that took the place of God's original design for His creation. This idol worship of self will crumble if we don't humble our flesh and trust God to do the work in us. If you want to heal without identity fettered to a fallen world, and you want to see the hand of God, stop worshipping yourself. God is telling an amazing story through your life. Start your healing by revealing the mysteries. God deserves all the glory, not us. Pride loves to hide behind labels. Pride truly goes before the fall! The old church's religious way is failing because love has grown cold. Many people remain silent about their faith or beliefs because they don't want to offend or lose any friendships, yet they judge most people "by their current fruit" and categorize their sins. It's time to look at sin and people's choices differently. It is not an identity! Just because someone drinks a little does not mean they are not Christian or not trustworthy. Just because someone cusses a little doesn't mean they should be avoided. We are all souls to be nurtured, not products to be measured. All people should have the opportunity to experience the Kingdom of God. He sees us and desires us.

Authenticity Matters

According to Peter Burke, "Identities tell us who we are, and they announce to others who we are." This statement has multiple interpretations. I believe: You are who you are, and there is hope that you can be satisfied with your I AM. When my daughter was a little girl, she hand-wrote and laminated a card that said, "I am who I am, and that's all I have to be." This marked a significant time in my life, as you will see toward the end. So, whatever you must go through to heal your identity, you will get the opportunity to share your testimony, with or without a label. The good news is you get to define your own label in creative ways based on your definition! So, what is true? Your identity is the story you tell yourself and the peace you have about your story! I moaned a lot about my life story and to the wrong people! As Joyce Meyer would say, 'go to the throne before you go to the phone.' She also said, 'You can have a moan-ey, or you can have a testimony.' Whatever you proclaim will be heard because words travel. What goes around the world comes back. I am a believer in the I AM, God of the Universe. He is the Almighty who created us to be in Him. The world you see is a choice. Choose the eternal loving identity so you can feel eternal peace.

If you cannot feel pleasure and joy in identifying underneath a particular identity label, then you can change. I was one who could not make up my mind. I wanted too many paths, and there is only one way if you want peace. Maybe you say, 'I am not at peace, and I don't feel joy.' While this may be true and valid, this should not become an identity based upon all your circumstances. As a close friend stated, "You must like your life because you are not changing. If you don't change, then you must find something comfortable about your life to stay there." It will take some time, maybe many years, to find inner peace, but first, let's discuss how people find identity and value.

Labels should not be harmful to our connections with society. People are identified when they are born, sometimes by race, sex, and name. Your place of birth, origin, religion, language, or any other cultural factor should not determine your value as a person. First impressions can be labels of identity that do more harm than good. Labels like Professional Baseball player, Christian singer, Female preacher, African American, political leader, Mexican Refugee, Wealthy, Poor, Georgia Bulldog Fan, and the list goes on. Social labels can often dictate the way we see both the world and us. This can often happen without realizing it. Our career titles may add confusion in this self-discovery labeling process, so it is important to think beyond that identity label. For example, a female diesel mechanic may have a hard time feeling her feminine identity among businesswomen. We are not the same person in a professional, religious, or ethnic setting, etc. Dressing comfortably or dressing in business attire should not change a person's confidence. At our workplaces, we tend to be more formal, responsible, attentive, and efficient as compared to how we act at home. Similarly, we behave differently at our churches, mosques, or synagogues. Labels like these should not affect our connections with world commerce, but unfortunately, they do.

My identity challenge was based on a falsely held performance identity, a poor foundation for measuring self-worth. I did not know how to define or measure "good enough". For many years, I compared my circumstances to others, and I made myself a victim of toxic thoughts. I was very hard on myself and felt like I could always do better. As a matter of fact, I struggled to feel accepted just as I was because I perceived myself to be rejected by others. Have you ever felt rejected because of the way someone judged your identity or value negatively? That's an example of how identity may begin to influence our emotions and thoughts in a way that might not always align with our initial feelings about ourselves. I am a person who is usually happy-spirited, but I was emotionally traumatized, and I changed. I lost my confidence and joy for a long time.

As a personal trainer, I'm under a magnifying glass all because of the label! It is awful to be judged, ridiculed, and cancelled from culture because of labels! This happens in careers, in homes, or with family. Try being in the insurance business or sales and often, you may feel rejection. As a trainer, if I were to drink wine and have chocolate mousse pie for dinner, I'm sure someone would say that I'm a bad example. My clothing, my career, financial status, my residence, my food choices, etc....may give facts, but they are not the truth about my identity. Identity identifications complicate the interpretation of our empirical world, which requires everything to be measured and documented. When a person fills out a form about their medical or employment history, he or she may aim to portray a perfect picture, but "that one area" separates you from the rest. I wonder how many of us may feel like we want to check the imaginary box: 'rejected, not good enough, never will be.'

I have found that identity attached to multiple areas results in mental discord against the unity of inner peace which we are meant to experience. Why do we want so much attention? Why do we need to be involved in so many jobs? I think it's because we want to be significantly chosen! The world will tell you, 'More is better.' This is why we are always trying to learn more and do more, but that's the problem!" More knowledge may increase your paycheck, but which knowledge you hold as truth will be the determining factor in your identity. In Hosea 4:6, scripture states that we suffer because of a lack of knowledge. The world will say, 'The more you are, the better you are.' As Alisa Keeton, owner of Revelation Wellness ®, states, 'More is not better, better is better.' I suffered because I was a people pleaser, trying to be a savior to everyone, learning, learning, learning! And guess what? I also gave away my peace. Had I kept my peace without the peer pressure of someone else's influence or judgment, I'm sure things could have worked out more peacefully. The trick of trade is to avoid thinking that you must save the world in order to be of significance and to matter. It took a while for me to learn, but I knew 'Superhero had to go!' It'll suck the life out of anyone, like a python grip! You can't be everything to everyone at the same time.

We envy more status, more money, and more time. Knowledge puffs up, and then we waste time and energy debating with others over the knowledge we call truth based on our newly established credentials or experience, just like the Pharisees arguing their truth with Truth, who was Jesus, standing right in front of them. The Pharisees' and Sadducees did not love Truth, they loved the law and judged others. They were proud and arrogant. They rejected the Messiah and did not enter the kingdom of heaven, even though they were so close! They couldn't understand how love could be grace and mercy. Surely those wise ones would be "the chosen among them all"!

Knowledge is different from wisdom. I believe Jesus is Wisdom, and those that seek Him will find Wisdom.[1] Just because someone is schooled does not mean they are skilled or that they have wisdom and discernment. The world has set a stigma label for job titles. Romans 12:3 reminds us, "Do not think of yourself more highly than you ought, but rather think of yourself with sober judgement, in accordance with the faith God has distributed to each of you." Our career pride may cause us to be critical, jealous, controlling, and negative based on material and emotional connections to this world (status'

---

[1] I Corin 1:18-2:16

like CEO, CPA, MD, etc...). As people grow older and wiser, they identify themselves less with other people, places, and things. They start to grow out of their initial selfishness or narcissism.

Role-playing is a form of identity that I struggled with, and it mentally and physically stressed me out for many years because it somehow connected to money. Although we are all human, our confidence is sometimes lost in a world of differing competencies. Role-playing is just part of living, and it's the function of wearing multiple hats in the world. Many of my 24/7 hats throughout the day went something like this: 4:30 am emergency wife, fitness instructor, mom, homeschool teacher, my husband's lunch assistant, Classical Conversations Director, wife, mom, karate instructor/student, Math teacher, wife. When my kids were in college, I was a fine dining server, self-employed gym owner, and my husband's accounting assistant. I'd guess my net worth was at least a 6-figure income per year! It was super chaotic when I felt the stress of wearing two or more of those hats simultaneously. I felt like all I did was "Whack-a-mole!" Your truest identity is the complete satisfaction of knowing who you are underneath the many hats or clothing. I struggled with my ego and the satisfaction of many titles, but I was not satisfied, especially if one of those areas suffered in performance output. It was like a toggle switch, on/off, or like a conveyor belt with a backup issue.

Identity per differing settings, naturally, is not alarming or hazardous for mental health, however, the extreme of anything could pose catastrophic threats to a person's identity, thus generating disastrous results. I have seen people who 'lost their identity' because they allowed victimhood, or what I call python eggs, in their heads. Maybe they were fired from a job, or their company went bankrupt. If one's identity remains culturally or circumstantially toxic with self-judgments based on status, personal choices, body image, or other external projections received, then love for self and others will grow colder, and the mental and physical health of that person may suffer. We do not perceive the harm we have done to ourselves or others. We learn the patterns of shame from others. Sometimes, we feel inadequate, or unworthy, but God always chooses us again and again, yet we discount ourselves as unworthy based on our works or regarding our current reality. This mental loss of identity could be just a temporal perception based on the five senses. If those external thoughts are not redirected, if we allow negative neurological patterns, we are also allowing a loss of peace and healing. Has shame and guilt controlled your life? Sometimes, we misperceive because we innocently do not know the freedom that may come from revealing the work of the Holy Spirit within us. Mental health issues can be resolved as we LET GO of the cultural pressures for performance identity and we begin to live more by the innate passion-filled calling on our lives. If the Spirit is not controlling the body, then an unhealthy body is controlling the mind.

The message of who I was got all twisted because of life's traumas, which start at a young age! Even the school administrators label students for their performance. It's no wonder kids fall into identity traumas. Many kids today are not free of guilt and condemnation. Comparing kids, segregating kids, and medicating kids could send a message to their minds about personal identity that they are not good enough and they need to do better. This comparison trauma became one of my pain stories, and my mind suffered due to trapped emotions. 'Sticks and stones may break my bones, but words will never hurt me' is a common false phrase. Toxic words we repeat to ourselves only solidify sickness. I struggled with a distorted kind of self-talk, like plucking a flower, "Love me, love me not." Approximately 80% of the American population labels themselves as *'not good enough'* because of the pressure to be perfect. According to Study Finds online, "An astounding eight in 10 flat out believe they are "not good enough" in virtually all areas of their lives." If we do not learn something from these unhealthy identities and start to choose to overcome them, we harm the world through our choices, attitudes, and behavior patterns. Mental health does not need a band-aid. We must start to deal with the root, not just pesticide the fruit! If depression medication could heal people, then why are over 37 million US citizens still taking it? The US is the most medicated country in the world. I believe the World Health Organization, ironically WHO, needs a Savior. His name is Jesus!

Sometimes, we get to a place in life where we need to "find ourselves." For two months, I trained a man who walked 500 miles for an entire month along the Camino de Santiago in Spain, a great hike to find yourself! He brought me a deck of cards. I shared these cards with several people in 2021, allowing people to randomly draw their own. My randomly drawn card stated: To live is to die! Finding myself also meant finding God within my life. In Phil. 1:21 scripture states, "To live is Christ, to die is gain." If we spend our days gaining the world, we could lose ourselves. We must be careful because mental health is on the rise.

The human experience of knowing myself started with

physical and personal relationships. My thoughts about my body and my values were broken and distorted before my late teenage years. I also developed an eating disorder called Bulimia in high school. The stress triggered me to binge, and then I made myself sick and took laxatives to purge the junk. Too many young people are stressing over things they should not have stressed about. Body image value may disrupt the way one connects with God. When I was younger, my identity was based on projections from other people as well as my own measure of my performance in activities including cheerleading and softball. This "love me, love me not" illusion in one's mind becomes their reality in the physical world, and it may not offer inner peace for finding "true identity" until later in life. I believe there is about a one-third chance for adults to develop this sound mind unless it was part of their foundation as a child. Maybe that's why Jesus said, 'Let the little children come to me.' Even children need spiritual instruction so they can become wise. When I was stuck between two thoughts, as Shakespeare quoted, 'To be or not to be,' I was miserable with a divided mind. Unfortunately, this "to be or not to be" is the common modus operandi. Double-mindedness is insanity! This should not be the case. The world is very unstable in relationships and those disturbances of the mind may last your lifetime. If we continue to practice being double-minded, this is unstable and mentally unhealthy. It creates a domino into our physical health. What will it take to be fearless, with a sound mind? Faith is risking the path of the One and Only Way!

    Every creation has value and purpose. Self-condemnation cannot align with faith in God's system of grace. Grace is not taught, yet it may be indirectly caught. Grace is God's gift in place of condemnation. Healthy living means letting go of toxic environments, people, and, mostly, --- Letting go of self-condemnation! You can do anything you want to do, just go at it with all your God-given strength. You are already worthy; you have nothing more to gain if you have Jesus. Go and share the good news!

I sense we all have worthiness issues at one point in life, and that's why we wear figurative Band-Aids. My healing story, without a personal identity attachment to the world, reminds me of people in the bible because it did not make sense that my life would be spared and would reflect the hand of God. It's a mystery. Healing the identity crisis comes by revealing your story! Who are we really? Are we just hiding? The first problematic issue is always referenced back to the Garden of Eden and the sin of the woman. Just like Adam and Eve, we know within ourselves, in our spirit, who we really are, but we get distracted by what others say or see in us. They wore fig leaves to feel more comfortable and protected in their circumstances, holding onto the fear of exposure to their choices. Some individuals are quite fine living inside their comfort zones, but that doesn't imply they're living their best lives. So why do the material goods make us feel more confident? Who told Adam and Eve to hide as if they were bad? I believe God, who is all-knowing, has had a plan for our redemption ever since creation. Maybe Adam thought Eve looked kind of cute in her fig attire, so she kept them on for entertainment later. Do you ever wonder if God is laughing at his creation because we do such silly things, like covering up what God knew was part of his plan all along? If Adam and Eve stayed innocent in their minds, I wonder if the message of Jesus would be taught from the pulpit of love instead of condemnation. Humankind has not changed much. Why are we so concerned about what others think? I don't believe John the Baptist was afraid to be the chosen one to lead the way. Appearance is overrated!

Who you are on this earth is symbolically like wearing a costume. It changes and may not fully satisfy you in every season. Halloween is a good example of hiding or finding comfort behind the mask. In 1995, my world started to unveil after the accident you'll read about in **Chapter Two**. The person underneath the costume is often a different person than who they are representing. Halloween night, the night of the devil's attack on our lives, I was a black cat who enjoyed flirtatiously teasing the dogs; however, the Alpha dog from Winn-Dixie who was dressed as a Budweiser woman, started to get jealous. Symbolic stories like Animal Farm by George Orwell. Symbolic stories like Animal Farm by George Orwell parallel the human tendency to rebel against oppression as the pigs did against Mr. Jones the alcoholic owner of the farm. When our protection is not healing, freeing, and transforming us, do we quit or push through?

I believe humans have an egoic spirit that wrestles against God. Jacob, the brother of Esau, wrestled with God to get his breakthrough. We must, spiritually speaking, go to war against our ego. Once we overcome the flesh, which is against God, we will transform. God gave Jacob a new name, Israel. It's almost as if we have dual personalities, and we need to find the one that frees us, the True Identity! As a human, you have the power to choose the spirit or the flesh, it's 50/50. If you choose the flesh, you are wrestling against yourself or others. Maybe it is a man wrestling with himself. Pride puffs up, and it becomes dangerous. Intelligent design against the wisdom from above is a battle between our flesh and our spirit. Our flesh operates in the natural world and could hurt us instead of freeing us. Our spirit operates in the supernatural world. To become One with the Creator, we must go deeper in our understanding of who we are and who others truly are. We are spirit in a body, not just a body with a spirit. Ephesians 6:12 states, "We wrestle not against flesh and blood, but against spiritual wickedness in high places." Because of this desire in our flesh, it is common to fall into believing lies. Our flesh wants approval, admiration, and acceptance. This is bondage. If you wrestle to free your spirit, you are wrestling not against the flesh but against spirits that want you in bondage. The thoughts of the flesh lead us down dark pathways without the light and awareness of God. Our inner critic may be the voice of our current direction. Often, the world's voices indiscriminately guilt us into believing lies about our life or identity. This voice we mistake as our source is the ego surfacing, and it is who we think we are. Possibly, we feel shame or some pain. In order to obtain freedom, try to listen to the One voice for the direction that leads to life and pray prayers that are for your good. The voices in the world can often be discouraging, but it's important to remember God's voice is the most important voice. Any voice outside of Him is usually pride or unbelief. Ask yourself, is it better to agree with God's plan, or your own? Scripture tells us to get understanding,[2] but this doesn't come by human reason. We may be wrestling, but we will overcome! In this book, you will hear the dual mindsets I experienced and how the Spirit works to free you from bondage. The voices that tell us who we are will always show up, maybe like a venomous snake in the

---

[2] Proverbs 4:7

garden or like a quiet, warm sunrise. The voice or image you choose to retain in your brain determines the hormones released as well as the patterns your brain is trained by. It's making a rut like a wheel in the ground for a trail. The trick is knowing which inner voice is telling the truth, the Way.

Your Choice Matters

I taught my kids, "If you don't choose, it will be chosen for you." Those choices have voices! Even the external voices may have power if you give them authority in your mind. The stronger voice wins! Listen for the correct voice! It's usually the soft one. Make no mistake, and there will be lots of voices – some internal and some external – that will question your significance or will put you through the misery of doubting yourself, hurting your self-esteem and your sense of self-worth, but you must overcome them. Be careful what agreements you make because some take years to remove! Unhealthy agreements need to be broken. Especially when you can't stop thinking about unhealthy shame and punishment mindsets. As a man thinks, so is he! Naturally, I am a bubbly, charismatic evangelical, so being who I know I am in every environment should feel limitless! Just like my daughter's limitless abundance mindset! I'm so proud of her and the discipline she has practiced to not conform to the patterns of the world and limited beliefs! Honestly, ask yourself, 'Am I confident in my identity, the one that is God-given? Or do I put my identity in any other form?'

We say money is not everything, but I see it all the time when people worship the power of it. I wanted to become a Physical Therapist, hoping this would solve all those financial fears connected with identity. Or at least the job title would satisfy my spouse and others who would be "so proud of me." I didn't want to have school debt since my parents could not afford much. Before college, I worked at St. Joseph's Hospital as a physical therapist tech, and one of the vendors noticed how impressive my work ethic was and he said, 'Wow, you need a larger title!' I replied laughing, 'Thank you, but more money would be nice! Psalm 23 reminds us that we shall not want, and he makes us lie down. Wanting something, like more money, would imply that you have a lack of money. While this may be a fact, if you lose your inner peace due to running after something that is not your true desire because of fear or lack, then you should consider turning around your thoughts as soon as possible. As a child, we did not have much money, but I never knew it. As a parent with more responsibility, I wanted more money but still battled with thoughts of losing valuable time, yet I felt insignificant without money. That's a lie! Yet I wore the Band-aid! It was a limiting belief, and I knew it had a hold on my heart. Beliefs about money will either keep you from releasing it or keep you from investing the pennies you may have to make your dreams come true. Money does not have power over God's authority to define who you are. Your value is priceless, without a price tag, paid in full!

You Matter

It's important to remember "You Matter," even when you feel like you are just the mom of your own kids. I always dressed in mom clothes, I had what some would call 'mom hair', and I drove a mom minivan. I did not always feel socially accepted. It's not about what's on the outside of you or your look that anoints you for greater things. Anointing does not always follow the good-looking standards of the world. Outer appearance can be deceptive. My Nanny had a personal conviction that you should dress up for church, but when I went to her church, she treated me like a soul. Her love was greater than the judgment about my casual clothing. I felt love from all her friends in her church. A soul, which is spiritual, cannot be measured or compared to the physical world because it is not a disposable product. Spiritually, we are who we are, and that never changes! Going to church can be difficult because of the inner critical voice in our head. Guilt is a heavy yoke. For the longest time, I lived based upon a record of wrongs against myself compared to others. Love keeps no record of wrongs. Learning to love and not judge requires right-mindedness. Wrong-mindedness is not the way to true joy. That's not living! You cannot heal when you focus on the wrong or painful path. It's like holding the thorn of a rose, expecting it not to hurt.

People's identity is rooted in their imaginary beliefs and in patterns that follow those beliefs. Who you are is also how you value the perception or imagination you retain in your brain at the time. This perception changes like the seasons. Often, people's perception leads to their projection. This is just another mind illusion. We want so badly to become the physical imagination we have for ourselves, and sadly we fall into worshiping the wrong things. Just like a cover label or book cover, the prideful person inside us wants attention and worship so that the attention is off Jesus. It's time to start imagining Jesus doing the impossible through you and take your eyes off yourself and all you must do to get attention from the world. If you live with shame, guilt, fear, unforgiveness, or other emotions that separate you from love and joy when you are doing the godly work, consider reading more of my story in **Chapter two** and **Three**. God literally did the work through me. His ways will lead you to abundance!

    Think about your identity without an identity label. It seems impossible not to label yourself, people, things, or events. You may call yourself a Christian, but then, when you are not perfect, you recognize that the label Christian is misrepresented. We mistakenly believed that the label Christian meant a representation of perfect. Oppositely, Christian just means you are a believer in Jesus. During hard times, my view of God was not loving or grace-filled. I did not allow myself to embrace self-love and approval because I wrongly believed I had to work harder and do better to receive love or any material blessing. Likewise, I believed that I was only blessed if I had faith. Identity is not work-based, and it is not all faith-based. It is love-based. You save yourself and others with the greatest gift, Love! When we are too hard on ourselves, we are also too judgmental toward others. Jesus stated in John 3:17, "For God did not send his Son into the world to condemn the world, but to save the world."

    It's better to trust your true identity, than it is to trust the presenting surface symptoms on the outside of us. Psalm 51:10 is a prayer I prayed because I had stored up the wrong beliefs in my heart, and I needed renewal. It says, "Create in me a pure heart, O God, and renew a steadfast spirit within me." It's always a good time to renew your heart toward God, no matter what excuses you may have for disobedience. You always matter!

Your DNA Matters

When I took the job as a math teacher at Strong Wall Christian Academy, I thought about myself, not my kids. This was an incredible opportunity to advance my education and training, but I was still operating on the wrong motive. I wanted to rise above the place I was emotionally experiencing. During my time there, I taught Pre-Algebra, Algebra, and Geometry to the private school kids. I may have experienced a fourth-dimension glimpse into the Spirit world, which my human mind could not comprehend since I was in a 3rd world density perspective. It was like God was literally connecting points of time for me when I could not see past the personal attack thoughts I felt in my life. He showed me some insight into the Golden Ratio. Everything is mysteriously put together in nature, including the divine design of our bodies. Did you know that the Fibonacci Sequence uses the last two digits to create the third? Here is the start of the sequence: 0, 1, 1, 2, 3, 5, 8, 13, 21, 34, 55, 89, 144, 233, 377, 610, 987, 1597, 2584, 4181. I could be imagining things, but look at the pattern: $1 + 1 = 2$ and $2 + 1 = 3$, $3 + 2 = 5$, $5 + 3 = 8$, and so forth. When we use our eyes to see and interpret the world on paper or by our own imagination, we only get a 2-dimensional or even 3-dimensional world. When we use our eye of intuition, the pineal gland, sometimes called our 3rd eye, we may see a world we didn't know existed because it goes beyond time and space. This impossibility is possible by the Spirit of the living God. Quantum Physics is just the beginning of this mystery! The Golden Ratio, the Fibonacci sequence, is 4th dimensional! I pondered this sequence and linked the story of 2 kids, my #5 story, married at age 21, Phi Delta sorority jersey #34. Then I also learned that the DNA molecule measures 34 angstroms long by 21 angstroms wide for each full cycle of its double helix spiral. These numbers, 34 and 21, are numbers in the Fibonacci series, and their ratio, 1.6190476, closely approximates the Greek letter Phi, 1.6180339. Mathnasium.com is a website that explains this Golden ratio, including the proportions of the human being, pinecones, ocean waves, and shells! Everything works together for our ability to see God's creation! We may not understand everything on this side of our humanness, but eventually, we will know God and all his creations will be unveiled to those who open or awaken! If you seek, you will find. Trusting God is the challenge we must overcome within ourselves.

Scripture states in Psalm 139:14 we are fearfully and wonderfully made. However, the word fear in this verse is not like fear as in scary, but it is fear as in awe and wonder! My name is written in the Spirit world, with God. He knew me before I was even born (Jeremiah 1:5). The immeasurable DNA from God is the code of life for you. We should not reject our make-up. As our worship pastor says, 'You get what you get, don't pitch a fit.' Your DNA may be hard to understand, because of the ability for gene expression; however, if you can avoid complaining about what you get, then you may see the blessing of its makeup. I like to think of myself like a turtle. I may have a hard shell, but I'm soft on the inside.

Your value is preset to "worthy" by the degree of Jesus' death. Although a human life is different from the food we eat, think about other valuable creations. The value of a chicken is the same as an eagle. It's how you look at it. Just like the value of all the jobs, yet they carry paradigm attachments in which we may assume a pecking order, aka a chain of command. Before we see the big picture and vastness of creation, like an eagle soaring above the birds, we may have pecked the ground like a mindless chicken eating a worm. The value of chicken when you think of feeding the world is priceless! The value of a garbage man is priceless. The value of a soul is priceless, too!

How a child is conceived and nurtured inside the womb will affect the nervous system's response to life beyond the womb. The brain-body is part of the central nervous system, one of the most valuable parts of the body. Just a couple of weeks after a child is conceived, the brain stem forms. Our thoughts travel through the nerves and may become trapped in parts of the body, causing disease or subluxation to the spine. Think about the effects of words and how they affect the expression of a person. I have recently taught myself not to attack my life source, DNA. It could stand for Do Not Attack. When someone does not feel love, they attack. I call this the Star Wars, the light versus dark side. Thoughts that cause offense, judgement, or retaliation toward others are attack thoughts. They are harmful, and we must be vigilant for life-giving thoughts. Thoughts become words. Words spoken are either life or death to the ears that hear.

Your Thoughts Matter

Our first thoughts about ourselves may happen in the womb. Our thoughts, words, and actions are setting up our destiny all the time. The mind, the will, and the emotions are a three-cord operation. Our thoughts are like the wind, changing all the time! It's what you do, energetically speaking, with that thought that determines the direction of your life. I believe the thoughts within the mind controls the brain to send the signals to the body, not vice versa. Thoughts come before the chemicals that are released in the brain. The brain and the eyes are the most complex mysteries of all creation, but I believe the mind can be programmed like a machine. If one can master the mind, one can guide their life experiences. It is said that to master anything, you must consciously and consistently practice the same pattern 10,000 times. Had I learned the power of repetition before my forties, I can only imagine how much emotionally further I would be! With patience, you learn who you are from the thoughts and voices you pattern yourself to listen to. We'll discuss thought training in **Chapter Three.**

"To know thyself" often references Socrates, the Ancient Greece philosopher. He also declared "that the unexamined life was not worth living." Some people hold tightly to a false belief about themselves and that is the reason they lose hope. Soul searching doesn't have to be a hopeless end. It could be exciting. It is a natural part of the life journey, and it is important. If there is no challenge, you may never experience change. To be born again is not just a rebirth like reincarnation. It is a change of mind. "Knowing thy self" is knowing truth by your innate intuition, a mystery you cannot measure. It's a gut feeling. It's not based on history. It's not like counting change as evidence. I think emotional freedom is evidence of God's love.

> *"You have to be your own person. You can't let people's opinions determine how you think about yourself. There's a difference between identity and self-identity."*
>
> – Amy Tan

Law of Attraction

Our identity is more about the agreements and attachments we make and how we perceive our life stories. Who you are will attract more of you, so be true to yourself. This is how social groups form. Likeness attracts likeness. Positive social groups or negative social groups. Google states, "The law of attraction states that you will attract into your life–whether wanted or unwanted–whatever you give your energy, focus, and attention to. You are constantly giving off vibrations of energy when you think and feel. These vibrations can be picked up and received by other people." The Law of Attraction claims we attract who we perceive ourselves or our lives to be. Isn't it interesting that in your body, the red blood cells know their identity groups and purpose, where to go and who to match to? Red blood cells follow other red blood cells! In other words, you attract more of who you are. The statement "misery loves company" is not to be taken lightly. I wish someone had taught me this before I created a mess in my mind! Cells multiply, just like crowds. Where one goes, another follows. I've heard it said, 'People are like cows, they herd together.' God has a plan for each of us, and he knows all things. Imagine this: You are a piece of a puzzle that belongs to the bigger picture. You try to fit into other pieces, "looking for that just right," and one day, you find your peaceful place. God knows you better than you know yourself. Your significance was predetermined before you were born, and He will make sure you travel to where you are meant to be.

I can relate to Peter in the Bible. Simon Peter, an apostle who lost his faith, declared himself weak and denied Jesus three times. Jesus forgave him and gave him "the keys of the kingdom of heaven," which represent the power of the Holy

Spirit within him. The keys to the kingdom are faith, hope, and love. The greatest is Love. God chose the humble, imperfect, uneducated and weak, and He gave them the opportunity to change the world. When Jesus called Peter the rock in Matthew 16, I thought to myself it certainly seemed like a foolish thing since he denied Christ. According to 1 Corinthians 1:27, "But God chose the foolish things of the world to shame the wise." He told Peter, after he had denied him in front of men, that he would build his church upon this rock. I'm sure Peter is just another example of how we struggle to comprehend how God could use a broken person with a hard heart. Rocks, like hard hearts, have many interpretations and usages in the scriptures. Unbelief is like a rock or a heart wall, where our hearts get spiritually hardened. It confounds me that God will use the person with mustard seed faith to move mountains (rock) and possibly to teach the proud and skilled. Not many apostles were educated, yet the scriptures teach us the foundations we need to live strong. The apostles were called, but not all were believers until they saw the evidence and answered the call by following the knock on their hearts before they had proof or confirmation of the way to go. They did not create their own way or wait for Jesus to come back and beg them to follow him. If you want to know the truth, you must follow the way that leads to miracles and mystery. See the Great Commission as stated in Matthew 28:19-20.

Your Calling Matters

Your calling is your mission, and some call it the purpose of your life. Each of us will be sent on a mission in our life, and I'm not talking about a mission trip to some 3rd world country. Sometimes, we will be blind to it, and God will keep knocking on the door of your heart until you open your heart. My first mission was to homeschool my children, and it took a while for me to hear that call. Before I committed to homeschooling our kids, I had a God moment. A year before it was time to send our daughter to public preschool, the Lord told me two words: Foundation and Village. My daughter went to a public pre-school while I worked as a personal trainer and aerobics instructor at the YMCA. One day, I was at a hip-hop workshop trying to obtain my CEUs for my group fitness certification at the YMCA. That day shifted the direction of my life. The Holy Spirit was pulling on my heartstrings. I could not stop crying. I left the fitness center due to uncontrollable emotions. As I drove across the bridge at Jimmy Carter Blvd, I was certain I had to homeschool! I called my friend from church who was also going to homeschool her daughter, and I told her about my recent experience. I described this overwhelming experience like Jesus before he went to the cross, in his prayer on the Mount of Olives, crying out to the Father, 'If you are willing, take this cup from me; yet not my will, but yours be done.' It was like a flood entered my eyeballs! Water represents the Holy Spirit. God was telling me to homeschool, and if I didn't follow in obedience, I would miss the anointing, and my kids would suffer because of my disobedience.

   As a stubborn person full of human ego wrestling between flesh and spirit, I struggled with the fear of making decisions, especially if they were counterculture. My husband and I had differing views about homeschooling. I worked at the YMCA and made wonderful connections with people who still remember and remind me of those awesome years. My workout friend from the ladies' gym, where I became an instructor, had a beautiful blue-eyed daughter and son close to our kid's ages. We would have Zaxby's after our workouts and let the kids play together. She told me that if I homeschooled, 'they will be social retards!' We must be careful of those external voices we rehearse. We do not want to rehearse a curse, taking on a false label. I was a mess emotionally until I answered the spiritual call toward obedience, fully surrendering my own might without fear that our kids would lack. Each morning, I said goodbye to my daughter for a few hours while she and her blue-eyed friend went to preschool. I remember my daughter's sweet little hands leaving my palms as I grieved at the idea of homeschooling her. Her hands have always been one of the silly things I love about her. I know God will use her hands one day to prophesy and heal people! I always told her she is blessed and highly favored! During the year before I answered the call, God often directed many homeschool moms in my path. Mysteriously, every week, I would meet another homeschool mom. I thought to myself, NO, I'm going to do personal training and plus, I'm not qualified with a teacher degree anyways. I certainly did not think, because of the school district or by confidence in myself, that I should homeschool. But God! Oh my God! He always wins, and that had to be okay with me! I decided to trust that God equips the called ME! I was becoming exactly who I was meant to be. My faith was exactly where it needed to be, fully relying on Jesus. I removed a Band-aid when I believed in God, not myself. I could hear the voice of God, and so I decided it was time to be obedient and surrender my personal plans. I chose not to align with fear or rejection, the lies and unbelief that my kids would be anything other than amazing. "To obey is better than sacrifice, and to heed is better than the fat of rams."³ God had a plan, so I put my trust in Him! Of course, in every anointing, there will be a devil's advocate, possibly as a mental reality. Unfortunately, at times, my husband did not feel confident I had heard from God about some choices I wanted to make. Bobby was not on the same page as me, so this battle was not won until there was proof. A war had to happen in the Spirit, and it was like a roller coaster. Some highs and some lows, like a heartbeat. I believe everything happens in the Spirit before it ever happens in the physical world. We must wrestle against culture, against change from the status quo, and against our own paradigms or fears. I never stuck with anything for a long time, possibly because I did not want people analyzing my life for fear that they'd find out about my weaknesses and I'd never succeed. I quit youth sports, Amway, AdvoCare, and College because of the limitations and beliefs I put upon myself.

The meanings we give identity labels may determine the speed of our potential. A great example is Paul of Tarsus. Everyone knew he persecuted Christians. When Saul was on his way to Damascus, a bright light blinded him for a period. He listened, and then he learned about God's plan for him. Likewise, as I put my trust in Jesus, he worked through me. Paul, an apostle of Jesus, had a thorn in his flesh, but the joy of his new assignment, which was setting the captives free, kept him from focusing on the thorn (pain of his mistakes). What we focus on grows. Never limit yourself by validating your weakness. I believe Paul learned to be a victor in Christ because he overcame the thorn of his sin, his past identity that tied him to a fallen temporal world. He just did what he was

---

[3] 1 Samuel 15:22 NIV

called to do and left the rest to God. I worried about my incompetence in carrying out my life's calling, but as a friend told me, 'That's God's problem.' If he calls you to a mission, then you have everything you need to bring it to completion. He equips the called, and he doesn't expect you to be equipped and then assigned or hired for the job. So many college trained individuals will tell you they felt like they knew little until they had experience in the field. You may not be called to reach the masses, but possibly you are called to reach one. Simple doesn't imply less satisfaction.

Your Name Matters

Names carry power! Saul's name was changed to Paul, which means small. Never underestimate God's ability to change the meaning of one's name. Paul wrote over half of the New Testament. Your name could be like a prophecy, believe it or not! Sometimes our name is the way we or someone else (through basic human understanding) labeled us to others. The question, 'Who are you?' is asked at a very young age when you don't even know who you are! You may know who you belong to, or what sex you were born as, or your name. For example, when I was a child, my Papa nicknamed me "Number Five" because I was his fifth grandchild. Mom said my middle name was "Trouble." Dad said I was "wishy-washy." My stepdad nicknamed me "Hot Shot." My college nickname was "LPS", for long, pointless story. My other stepdad called me "Jumping-Jack Flash." Today, I'm called "Coach." Names change and have different meanings all the time.

When I was a tween, I started playing softball, and I can remember people calling me a boy. Why do looks and names affect our beliefs about ourselves so much? Hair does matter as a form of identity in this world. Why is that okay? Is this normal? In middle school, I remember having a crush on a football player who had a girl's name, and his jersey was number eleven. He was fit and healthy, something I thought I wanted in a guy. Even my mother was trained to obtain one that looked good and that's one reason she felt pressure to marry my dad. One weekend, my dad came to pick up my sister and me for his weekend. It may have been an identity challenge for Dad to see our hair cut off, but it was not Mom's fault that the hair stylist thought I had lice. Dad barely recognized us with boy-short hair. I labeled myself as a tomboy with that boy haircut starting my teen years, playing softball with all those wild hormones that confuse identity.

We often identify with the meanings of our nicknames or the origins of our names. My boyfriend's first name, Bobby, was certainly ironic! Names are like genetic codes. My grandmother was faithfully married to a man named Bobby. My mother married a man named Bobby. My boyfriend had similar issues that connected a similar story to both my grandmother's and mother's experiences with alcohol. My first name means heart, and my married name means brave heart. Our future together could be unfolding a God connection: a double-hearted treasure. Within the heart is treasure emotions, and it is sacred. We hold onto our emotions! "Where your treasure is, there your heart is also."[4]

My son's name means candlemaker, and today, he is an electrical line worker. My daughter's name means God is my teacher! According to an online source, nameberry.com, there

---
[4] Matthew 6:19-21

are 12 names that mean salvation, some include Jesus, Jace, Joshua, Elisha, and others. One may make a connection that Jesus is Jehovah, the Lord, the Messiah, our Salvation! Who is Jesus? He identified as "I AM." He was the perfect innocent Lamb of God! He was perfect, right? Born to a perfect family, right? Well, according to tradition for a king's appearance and wealth status, he was not perfect to the standard of the times for a king! Think for a moment. Born to a poor family, in a manger, and laid in an animal trough! Doesn't that sound impressive? Nope! Jesus was not just a carpenter's son from Nazareth. He was and is the Messiah. Although the Jews could not understand this, he walked in confidence without having to prove himself. Humility was his best trait! Jesus asked, "Who do you say I am?' Peter replied, "You are the Messiah." Jesus responded, "This was not revealed to you by flesh and blood but by my Father in heaven." When Moses, who felt the pressure to save the Israelites, doubted the power given him, he asked the Holy Spirit the question, 'who should I say sent me?' The response was, 'say I AM sent you.' Moses stood before the burning bush, which spoke audibly. We could be like that burning bush filled with the Spirit of the living God, kind of like a lighthouse upon a hill, or we could flame so furiously that we damage lives around us. A person's "true" identity is God-given; however, I believe surface-level identity is never one's "true" identity. It's much deeper than appearance.

Your Innocence Matters

If all sin is forgiven by the blood of Jesus and we are innocent, then our perspectives toward ourselves and others could be more about trusting God in the pruning process. It's like we are gardens, and at times we have weeds. This is normal. When I was a child, I thought like a child. Even as an adult, I behave like a child! The discovery stage of a child begins with the questions: Who, what, when, where? It's interesting to me that I spent most of my life asking WHY? My foundations were out of order. Children are so innocent! Who could ever reject such innocence? Yet, this happens every day! Our children are conforming to our patterns; they are catching what they are seeing. When the child asks 'Why?' This is a perfect opportunity to take the time to explain, but we underestimate the ability of a child to understand. The common reply was, "Because I said so!" This taught me two things: either shut up and obey or do it anyway. I learned the rebellion way and probably needed more spankings. That was still accepted as correction in the 80s. When a parent can discipline in love, they are teaching a child the way they should go. This way, obedience is not forced!

When I became an adult, I was still learning from my misunderstandings, and I was still innocent by the testimony of Jesus Christ. He said in Luke 23:34, "Forgive them. They know not what they do." As you read further along, imagine sin is just like being blind. People are blind until God awakens them. Before my salvation, I was blind. Even after my salvation, I was a Pharisee, blind to my own sin. I was just a product of my environment when I was blind. Are we, not all just role-modeling what we see in other adults? People are hurting from misunderstandings or misinterpretations of sin. This is what causes us to have unbelief. This sin hinders the healing process. Jesus is the true healer because he forgave sin. As 1 John 4:18 declares, "There is no fear in love. But perfect love drives out fear because fear has to do with punishment.

The one who fears is not made perfect in love because he still believes in punishment and condemnation."

At a young, innocent age, I lacked understanding of love and the grace Jesus blessed us with. I didn't know what I was doing. I was normal. I had a boyfriend because that's what kids in grade school do, right? So, by fifth grade, I French-kissed a boy! Nowadays, that is not a big deal. Later, I learned that I had opened a door for lust, and shame was right behind it. Sadly, the kiss felt too good to never kiss a boy again. I attracted a lot of attention, and this started an addiction to "I'm somebody!" But that label got me into a lot of situations. This irritated my sister! Just for laughs, people would ask, 'Who's your boyfriend this week?' Performance was always easy for me, and obtaining a boyfriend was, too! There was a jealous spirit between us growing up, but God corrects those he loves. I was an insecure female due to circumstances and all the distractions, like lust, when I needed true love. We all fall short of the glory of God. At a young age, I didn't sin much; therefore, my need for a Savior was minimal. When one believes in Jesus, they are said to be saved. To be saved means a change of mind. Before the age of eleven, I was saved and baptized in the Baptist church, but that did not make me a perfect Christian. Verbal confessions without heart transformations throughout your life experiences can lead to toxic Christianity. The devil often attacks the church, the believers of Jesus, because they are anointed. When a believer is anointed, their light is bright! I was not discipled by believers at a young moldable age. Oddly, I don't remember much of my childhood before age eleven. By the time I was ready for high school, we had moved five times. It was only by pictures and the retold mysteries from my sister do I even recall a mist of those earlier years. Maybe my mom prayed I would forget? I was eleven years old when my stepdad labeled me an A-hole for asking him when he was going to stop drinking alcohol. If looks could kill. I started dying because I felt I was a bad person for asking questions. This broken spirit was the devil's assignment. Like playing dominos, everything is connected! God connects all our pieces into one big story!

Only God knows why we do the silly things we do, and it is in this life that we have been given the opportunity to know God and make him known. Love is a huge struggle! Love is a spirit, and hate is a spirit. It's a strange phenomenon, but it is true: your greatest struggle will be your greatest victory. Ownership for who you say you are has no one else to blame. I decided it was time to seek and find inner peace. We must surrender to find freedom and experience the miracle of truly living, not just existing. Our unique calling or purpose confounds most people. For me to learn more about my identity meant taking inventory of my experiences. In 2022, I enrolled in the Unique program, which helps people look at their lives and see how God has been telling His great story all along. My story is a piece of the universe God made for us to experience.

Your identity can be your choice. How can we make sure we are making the right decisions that are in alignment with God's will? His will is for you to live satisfied in knowing who you are. Jesus was absolutely and confidently himself in God and he didn't need to label himself with any ties to the world. He wants us to know who we are because who we are says a lot about the peace we experience on earth. Who Am I? This is a question that most of us seek to find the answer to while we still have time on Earth. My Nanny said, "As long as there is life, there is hope." Casting Crowns and Matthew West have a song called *"Nobody"* and this is truly an incredible song if you are a deep thinker! Jesus came as a nobody, without a biological earth father and without a generalized label. He did not classify himself as a carpenter's son from Nazareth, which may imply a lesser status. When it was time for Jesus to start his ministry, the power to forgive sins and heal every disease came upon him. New energy reigned over many who wanted their disease healed. Dis-ease is exactly that, a separation from your peaceful confidence in Christ. You are not your disease, so do not absorb disease into your conscious. Reconceptualize the term and find the value in what the world would call a weakness. I chose to become a Nobody. This was so freeing for me! If you can value a Nobody to the world, you will find healing, freedom, and inner peace with your identity. Nobody is the most significant to Jesus. He spoke to and touched all the Nobodies without fear! I desired to learn that being a nobody allowed the ONE and ONLY somebody within me to rise as well, and this same power is available to anyone who believes in Jesus. Christ could be the foundation of our identity - not our job, our possessions, or what others say about us. The convictions we have about ourselves change based upon personal choice, beliefs, practices, programming from the world, or possibly from one's traditional or generational heritage. Our satisfaction will be tested because of our selfish and judgmental nature.

People want to make Jesus into a nobody, making Him the last source, but to some, He is Hope! Ironic, right? It's completely fascinating to those who can see the mysterious God in all of creation. As it says in Psalm 19, "the heavens declare the glory of God." This hope in Jesus is a vital part of human existence, as we cannot survive without some type of hope. However, hope would not be possible without faith. Faith gives reality to our hopes. What or who you believe in is often born from an inheritance of previous experience, or it is transmitted to us by the Word of God. Faith becomes an image of the hope you have in whomever or whatever, and this vision will direct your obedience or allegiance. Your Choice matters! As Deuteronomy 30:19 states, "Choose Life so that you and your descendants will live." Chasing after meaningless things is the path to losing your identity. Your reward is in keeping to the faith that you are Chosen, Called, and Commissioned for greatness in Christ.

Chapter Two
For me, not against me

> *"And the God of all grace, who called you to his eternal glory in Christ, after you have suffered a little while, will himself restore you and make you strong, firm, and steadfast."*
>
> *-1 Peter 5:10 (my birth verse)*

In your suffering, do you ever feel like God is not with you? Deep in the pit, Joseph may have felt abandoned, but I believe he knew his destiny was beyond the hopelessness of the pit. When your life reflects more fear than faith, you are suffering. Fear of uncertainty, fear of rejection from others, or any form of separation could keep you from overcoming a toxic mind. A fear problem can be solved through the relationship we have with Jesus and each other. We don't solve the problems when we hide or run away because, unfortunately, it is like a shadow. it follows you. Remember the children's bear story, "We're going on a Bear Hunt!?" The lyrics state, *"You can't go over it, can't go under it, you gotta go through it!"* The last line is, 'Let's not go bear hunting anymore'. We may question our direction because of distractions or evil in the world, but God will take what the enemy meant for bad, and he'll turn it around for your good. Trust the scripture, Romans 8:31: "If God is for us, who can be against us!"

My parents divorced a day before my fifth birthday, which, of course, had many consequences. Maybe internally, they made an agreement that their love was not strong enough to create a healthy relationship for my sister and me. Choices have consequences, kind of like cause and effect, but I have decided not to blame their choice for my life struggles because personal ownership is an important first step to the realization path for freedom. Yes, divorce brings about legal, financial, emotional, and practical issues that necessitate time, energy, and a shift in responsibility. It might take years for individuals to restore their equilibrium for emotional peace. Nonetheless, divorce serves a vital legal and emotional role. I don't believe their separation was a mistake or that they should have any regrets. Everything that happens is always an opportunity for us to see a treasure or blessing in disguise. Think for a moment of a sunken treasure box. There are always more treasures among the broken locks. If love is not able to flow freely, then the treasures get stored up, rusted, and decayed. It's about what is inside the treasure that can either destroy you or give you an opportunity. We are not free when we hide and store up things we are afraid others will find. What I mean is this: the things we wish no one knew about can most likely be the healing we need. If we want fear to cease, love must not be contained. Love for yourself and others must be free to flow. Without the freedom to love, we have issues stored up in the heart. Some say hate is the opposite of love. Actually, the opposite is fear, which hurts the world. Maybe they just had a common fear that things would not work out well if they stayed together. The transition of divorce can bring a rollercoaster of emotions for the whole family, and that includes the children. They may feel a range of intense emotions such as loss, anger, anxiety, and confusion. Divorce can leave children, even adults, feeling overwhelmed and emotionally sensitive in future relationships. Especially at the age of five, it can be scary for a child. Divorce brings many uncertainties. Uncertainty may be a strong feeling, whereas certainty always feels much better. There is no absolute certainty in the time we are here on this earth. If we can become comfortable with the fact that uncertainty is part of living, then we won't have to suffer from the effects of worry every day. A friend told me that worry is a belief that God will mess it up. Can God mess up? I don't see any evidence that God messed up when he created me. I messed up when I created beliefs that were not true. Thoughts retrained generate stronger neurological pathways for healing. Nothing is wasted. My Nanny always held a special place in my heart. She said, "Honey, if you are worrying, then you are not trusting, and if you are trusting, then you are not worrying."

At times, my worry turned to fear. This is a powerful feeling that may keep individuals from moving ahead in their lives. Fear and control go hand in hand. When we allow fear to take over, we close ourselves up to new opportunities and experiences or relationships that may enrich and fulfill our lives. The Holy Spirit is grieved if we close ourselves up to these opportunities. When you're living in fear, you're unable to think with abundance or think clearly and rationally. This leads us to distorted views and poor judgment calls. In general, fear can have several negative consequences on your ability to make healthy judgments. It's also easier to imagine threats that don't exist when you're overwhelmed with fear. Making decisions becomes difficult when you have deeply wounded emotions that are often misinterpretations of God's plan for your life.

Whether we experience little traumas, like our parents' divorce or big traumas, it is still an experience that needs to be processed through the body. My sister and I were latch-key children because Mom had to work a lot since child support was not always dependable. In my later years, I almost repeated what is common to culture (divorce), but God would not let me choose that path. He taught me many lessons through long-suffering.

As a method for healing, some people go to therapy, play sports, and/or go to church. Whatever works well for you to heal is what matters. Exercise is recommended for emotional healing, but exercise alone may not solve the trapped emotion or trauma from divorce or any other form of rejection. My mom wanted both my sister and I to be involved in activities that could help us emotionally and socially. I loved playing softball; it made me feel tough! My dad coached my softball team. As an adult, I took up karate with my kids for ten years.

Now, I am a fitness trainer and exercise six days a week, but this is only about 20% of my mental therapy. The other 80% I would propose is a much deeper issue, deeper than a feeling or an event. We must look at the whole picture to truly heal from trauma. My parents were hurt by the church, and so turned away from their so-called hypocritical help. The only one who is not a hypocrite is Jesus, and he never wavered in unbelief. Although my parents did not choose church as their main guiding source when my sister and I were kids, they did maintain peaceful relations, so we were not further traumatized. I learned a lot about parenting from my mother, and I'll forever be grateful for her. No one can possibly be perfect, but she did her best for my sister and me. As a result of the separation, a form of guilt or jealousy may have influenced my mom's decisions and wishes for us to have a better life. All they knew to do was to live day by day. This is great advice. Be present with each day, with an attitude of gratitude. As Zig-Ziglar quotes, "Your attitude will determine your altitude." Yes, attitude! How we speak, look, or behave in our circumstances will affect our position. One thing for certain is to never compare your parents or anything in judgment against another. It always causes drama and hurts one or more people.

Do you think you have a perfect family? Due to Facebook, we assume everyone except us has a perfect family. Consider a child's drawing of their family, and the confidence he or she has knowing who each figure with no neck and no arms represents. You might tell the child, 'Wow, it's a beautiful, perfect family picture!' The common person would accept it and then comment to others (hoping the child would not hear the criticism) about the missing parts or need for improvements. It's the gossip seed! I believe some things are better when we keep our mouths shut and watch for those God moments or opportunities to bless these little innocent children to never compare their image to another person's image. Why complain or make critical remarks? We can easily crush the spirit of a child because we do not think before we speak. Learning to respond like Jesus is important.

Your Words Matter

Words have energy, and when they penetrate the walls of the heart, change is possible. Maybe a hard heart is not easily penetrated? In the book Charlotte's Web, E.B. White is quoted, "With the right words, you can change the world." In the book Animal Farm, George Orwell writes about the animals who make their own farm rules to flip the governing power. If the language is interpreted with a different perspective, then an entire community can shift the dynamics of authority, as the animals did. Our words are setting into motion people and events. It is said that if one can change the language of a nation, he can rule the nation. That's how propaganda works. Marketing is manipulation. We must pay close attention to how words are used. Our words can be molded by the acronym KNIT. Are your words kind, necessary, important, and timely? I most definitely had faults in this area! My brother-in-law taught his boys, 'You are not a Christian by the way you act. You are a Christian by the way you react.' Reacting with a proper unoffensive response if you are rejected can be practiced (modeled) until it feels authentic, but this takes time to develop, and we are not patient with ourselves or others in this journey to become who we truly are. Even as an adult, I have crushed the spirit and faith of others, even my own faith, because I did not think about what God could do in a situation before I spoke out my feelings. I forgive myself for such foolishness. I just didn't know the impact of my words or my actions because I was not always walking in the Spirit. And who is always walking in the Spirit, except God, right?

Your Destiny Matters

Important people are meant to come into your life. Destiny may be connected with pre-destination, as if everything that happens is meant to happen. When my father met my stepmom, my sister and I started to develop a relationship with my dad again. This was an opportunity for Thanksgiving! She always included my sister and me as much as possible so we wouldn't lose our relationship with our dad, who was very involved with his career as an upholsterer. I'm proud of his 50-plus years of commitment to serving as the best in his field. He crafted with his innate skills and had a keen eye for detail. The ideas he implemented were perfectly translated from his imagination into craftsmanship. I remember working with him at his shop and going to Dunkin Donuts for a warm blueberry muffin and a tab of butter on top of the crystallized sugar. Though my parents' divorce felt like it was against me, I know God had a plan for my sister and me to have two wonderful half-siblings. They are living their best lives as adults now. When they were young, my sister and I were included to go on snow skiing adventures, the beach, and their backyard pool. As my children grew up, Mom and her current husband took us camping. And, we went on several Dollywood and pontoon boat trips. All the memories are treasures made in love!

We can open ourselves up to the signs and miracles around us if we don't focus on self-pity when we are on an uncomfortable path, such as a pit. Joseph went from the pit, when his brothers sold him for money, to the kingdom with lots of money, giving him the ability to help many of God's people, including his brothers who abandoned him. It's common to go through life blaming others for the pitiful life you go through, but it's a whole lot wiser if we shift our perspective and see the circumstances we face as happening "for us" instead of against us. We may feel like we are at the end with no hope, but we gotta' get out of it somehow. Just like Joseph, the 'dreamer' and son of Jacob, thrown into a pit to die but set up for a miracle. Remember this, God sees it all, and Joseph was the one who was given favor! If you remember the story, he had a coat of many colors! I imagine that this coat could represent many nations. If you think about it, there are no colors that are left out of the kingdom of God.

There is a story about a farmer whose horse fell into a large pit. Symbolically like the devil, the farmer decided to bury the horse alive. He began shoveling dirt on top of the horse. Now, according to the farmer, the horse was not too smart. It would not surrender to death. The horse ignorantly kept picking up its feet, day after day, without any food or water. The farmer went away and returned to find the horse was still alive, way down in the pit. He had wished the horse would just die. There was no salvation for him. He was mad that the horse would not give in to the dirt! Again, the farmer attempted to bury the horse. After months of shoveling dirt on top of the horse, the horse saved himself one step up at a time! The horse made it to the top!

This story has helped me get through life. I realized that my salvation was not in someone physical or external to me, but it was within my own faith to overcome the internal problem. I had a problem of self-doubt and even meditated on taking my life because I became mentally hopeless, always measuring and comparing myself. When I felt like life happened to me, I felt the deep, painful emotion of depression, and I would often blame someone for the circumstances of my choices and inadequacies. Instead of getting out of that illusion of the pit, I would attach to some form of culture, trying to gain significance through people and jobs. When we think our circumstances must change, then we'll be happy. We have it backwards. First, you must dream and visualize your salvation. Wounds and bad things happen. We Band-aid it and continue living, thinking this is normal but everything has a purpose that it may make you stronger. My marriage made me stronger; it gave me opportunities to pray. When God calls you to be who you were meant to be, and he sets you free from bondage to yourself, then LISTEN and LEARN! Delayed obedience doesn't have to be bad news or create any shame. As Nike would say, "Just do it!" Our training may be painful, but the Lord knows what it will take to get your attention. Over time, you will learn to focus less on the pain, and you'll begin to see the hand of God.

Miracles happen every day, but no one wants to be in a place of needing a miracle. They happen when the odds are against the possibilities, and then people lean into faith. Just think a moment--if people leaned into faith, we could be experiencing outcomes that could blow our egocentric minds into another realm! The miracles are the odds left in God's hands. He can handle our broken hearts. If your heart is broken because of events which you felt were against you, you may be in a place of needing a miracle.

The Mystery

Miracles started to happen in my life at a young age. This miracle helped me see God is for me, not against me! This was the first car accident when God protected my life! My mom did not choose to have a car wreck on 9/9/89, nor did she choose that my sister would move in with my dad and stepmom before the wreck because she didn't agree with mom's choices. Mom and her friend were leaving the football game in a large pickup truck from the high school that I would be attending the following year. It was late, but they wanted a brownie from Applebee's restaurant. I was supposed to ride home with them, but I left the game with my friend. A man drove through a red light and struck the truck on the passenger's side. Mom broke her hip in three places, and her friend practically had his arm ripped off to save my mom from flying through the front windshield (seatbelts were not installed). I would not have survived the impact if I were with them seated on the passenger side; it was that tragic.

Fortunately, I had altered my ride home. Life is unpredictable, just like a football game. You might have some unfortunate setbacks, or you may have to create some different strategies because you feel like you're losing at halftime, but it's not over until the final whistle blows. You can't give up in the middle of the game or in your 40s. Everyone has a purpose on Earth, and you won't be able to fulfill yours until God, and you see it through to the end. Feeling helpless at such an uncertain time is natural. But if we stay emotionally stuck and don't move forward, we're only doing more internal harm on our bodies.

It was tough to witness their rehabilitation after the accident. My mom and her friend went through months of pain. During that time, I worked hard to graduate with high honors from one of the top high schools in the state. As a reward for my hard work and dedication to helping them every day after school, I was able to go on a cruise to the Bahamas with my high school best friend a couple of years later. Along with that, I also became a certified scuba diver and went on many scuba diving excursions. The experience with my mom and her friend helped me realize that I wanted to become a Physical Therapist so that I could help others who were going through rehabilitation. I started a future vision for myself, but I became distracted.

In the summer of 11th grade, I met an attractive guy at Winn-Dixie, my first real job (not a babysitting job). I mindlessly forgot all about the guy I had been with for the past two years, who was expected to go into pro baseball. He was perfect in my mom's eyes, but I did not have that same feeling toward him. Each person has a divine plan and a calling in their life, but at times, it may feel like puzzle pieces that don't fit well. With lots of questions, people plan their lives according to what they desire to do, but if they don't get what they desire, they may feel frustrated. Given enough time, eventually, the puzzle pieces of life fit together. I believe the baseball player my mom liked was not the chosen person for me.

Stubbornness, rebellion, control, independence, and charisma! That was me! Trouble! I never chose the direction of obedience and alignment with normalcy. I think God loves to use people like me and the Winn-Dixie boy because we are a challenge to change. The story with the attractive guy from Winn-Dixie fits the puzzle of life for me. He became another life experience. A good story has a villain and a hero, right? Would this new guy be the villain or the hero? I love the kind of stories with a plot twist. The mysteries unveil (like a Broadway curtain) at the right time. When the villain finally hears, outside of his own prideful ego, he becomes the hero!

The day I met that hot guy will never be forgotten. My heart thumped a new beat! This magnet male model, a diary department manager, hooked my attention, coming through my checkout line with pizzas for the guys. Was I blind? Where was he when I started working there six months before?

"Who are you buying those pizzas for?" I asked.

Clueless to my flirtatious question, he responded, "It's Spring Break, and I'm just hanging out with my friends."

"Well, maybe you can save one of those pizzas for us!" I winked.

The winking of the eye causes trouble. See Proverbs 10:10 ESV. I knew it was wrong, but I could not stop flirting with him. I had a perversion spirit from past generations that was harvested in my teenage years. I noticed this guy had muscles, long hair, a tan, and blue eyes. Oh, he was so attractive and still is but I see him differently now that I am delivered from this spirit. In 1993, I started an intimate relationship with him as soon as I returned from the beach. We were attracted to one another physically. Previously, I had opened the Pandora box with the guy I was dating (the baseball player). The Pandora box is the box of "What if?" This box spoke to me in times of insecurity and soul-searching. The peer pressure in high school to have sex got the best of me. If I didn't 'do it' before I was married, then my wedding night would not be exciting. I believed the deception, 'What could it hurt to do it one time? Because of my own insecurities and the societal labels which I imagined in my head, I made a snap decision that ended up costing me something valuable: my virginity. I felt distant from God, and this feeling affected my sanity and peace of mind. Sin has consequences, no doubt. Fornication is common, and it is the common things (things we are absent-minded about) that we fall into. I gave the baseball player a piece of my life puzzle, which I could not redeem. I had to abruptly end the relationship with the baseball player because I knew my affection for this new guy was not right towards the other guy. Breaking someone's innocent heart hurts. I wanted to "know" Bobby now that I had experience with sexual pleasures. I enjoyed the dark, secretive thrill of life with Bobby.

Our lives are not messed up although we think we've messed up our lives with all the sins and mistakes we make, but I believe God sees it all and will not let us fall when we trust him. There will be a time of darkness, but the light is coming! Daniel 2:22 states, "He reveals deep and hidden things; he knows what lies in darkness, and light dwells with him." Job 12:22 also references the darkness, "He reveals the deep things of darkness and brings utter darkness into the light." I believe we must go to the deep, get the sunken treasure, break the lock, and 'search out a matter.'[5] But "there is a God in heaven who reveals mysteries."[6]

At age sixteen, I picked out an affordable car. My first car was an automatic Chrysler Labaran convertible, for which I paid half, and Mom paid the other half. My boyfriend had an exact one, but his was black! Based on my decisions, mine should have been black. After two years, I broke up with him for Bobby. Bobby, the Winn-Dixie guy. Although Bobby did not live by the bible, he was funny poetic, and he knew a lot about fixing cars. Just a few weeks into our relationship, I was smoking weed and continuing pre-marital sex! That's stupid! Not saying all people are stupid; I just wasn't thinking, and that is how I labeled myself! I did not do much thinking about my life choices.

Before our first date, he wanted to introduce himself to my mom, but I knew she would not let me go out with him because he smoked cigarettes, so we scurried out. The sound of his red Ford Escort muffler could be heard from over half a mile away, so I was already ready to leave. At the time, I was not convicted of my sin because I wasn't filled with the Holy Spirit and awakened to God's grace. When we think we are above God or our parents and we hide our sins, eventually, all things will come to the surface. I did not know about soul ties and generational curses. We may have started a relationship

---

[5] Proverbs 25:2 NIV

[6] Daniel 2:28 NIV

based on lust and a broken foundation. Sexual sin was a root or possibly a curse to our first connection. Everyone searches for love, but unfortunately, love is distorted through many images, even pornography. I was looking for love, but I didn't know true love. God is love, but I didn't really have a true love for myself, others, or God. Deception entered my heart.

Mom was not happy with my decisions, but she knew I was going to do what I wanted to do regardless of what she wanted for me. I was a typical rebellious teenager. She reluctantly allowed me to get away with things because she picked her battles with a larger perspective. My mom was doing her best to keep me from trouble, but she knew that controlling me, based on her religious experiences, would only make me more rebellious. Mom did what she believed was best at the time, even when she probably wanted to choke me. I remember this conversation between my mother and me like it was yesterday:

"Whose cigarettes are these?" Mom asked me after opening the glove compartment in search of a repair document.

"They are mine, mom!"

"Surely, I've taught you better!" Retorted my mom!

Wanting attention, I had it at that point! She knew she raised me to think, or possibly, she had hopes that God would correct the error of my ways, which he does so patiently and gently! Mom's perspective of others, without being too religious about any issue, helped me to have friends in every social class. She always tried to help me see other's perspectives, even if they were seemingly not the best view to withhold. My mom trusted me, prayed for me, and loved me as much as she knew how to love. As any mother would, she worried about my choices. Truly, I was her last kid for a good reason. I questioned everything and always asked, "But why?" She would reply, "Because I said So!" Mom tried hard not to get frustrated with me.

Bobby taught me how to drive his car with a 5-gear clutch. Innately, he knew I loved a challenge! He parked his red Ford Escort on a hill and traded seats with me. The challenge was to keep from rolling backwards into the car behind us at the stop sign. I surrendered my fear about the challenge, and I made it up the hill without a crash.

He is very brave, and God has shown him grace and unconditional love many times! On one night shift at Winn-Dixie grocery store, as an Assistant Store Manager at age 18, he had to avoid being killed in a robbery. God protected him! He also spared him in high school at his football game when he drank too much. He also survived a coma when he mixed ephedrine with alcohol before he competed in a wrestling match. Bobby attended a rival high school, and he had just graduated when we started dating. Little did he know, but I had control and security issues, fear about my future, and fear about my competence to do well financially on my own. I questioned, 'Would this guy like me because of who I would become? I wasn't a "goody tu' shoes" church girl or the one with money. I was just a cute cheerleader who loved attention. I did not do drugs or party much. My mom raised me with moral ethics. I went to good schools, and sometimes we went to church. I pretended to be Holy but was not whole. I hid my sin well. Who was I hiding from anyway? Who was I really? Remember the picture book by Craig Sidell, *The Life and*

Times of Fuzzy Wuzzy. He teaches us to look beyond external matters. Externally, he had no hair, but his name described him as Fuzzy. The name Christian means nothing externally until the internal self is transformed, and that takes time. Sometimes I feel like my life is becoming so exposed, hairless, that I don't even recognize myself anymore. It's almost humorous!

Are our steps truly ordered by the Creator? We are both Taurus, so that didn't match! I met his family, and his mom shared her thoughts about me, 'Oh no! A cheerleader!' However, she was super kind and accepted my presence, even early in the morning when I visited before school. Bobby had good looks and a Christian home, which seemed like the perfect match! I thought his family was not broken like mine because they went to church, and his parents were still married. Bobby's mother was always praying in a language that sounded like gibberish. I was fascinated by the fervent, energetic prayer coming from the upstairs back room. I'm sure her prayer language was changing some generational curses because that's what spiritual language does. Language changes nations and opens prison doors! He told me not to pay any attention to that and just come to his room. I remember thinking, 'How in the world did I get myself to this strange place?' A Christian home with strange practices. His mom, a true and faithful believer, probably knew what we were doing behind closed doors, so she would enter without knocking and begin to vacuum his room! She innately knew we were in darkness. That's what the spiritual world is like! A door! We open spiritual doors to either the dark side or the light side. Bobby and I united to become one flesh in a sense behind closed doors.

Bobby and I were living on the outside edge of morality.

The summer before his major life-altering accident, we went to a party intending to drink underage and celebrate graduation with friends. I remember a mysterious lady of wisdom caught my attention. I don't know who she was, but that's when the spiritual scales on my eyes began to drop, and God planted a seed of right-mindedness in me. I do not remember her face, but I was drawn to speak with her for over an hour. She recognized an anointing I did not know I carried within me. I was captive to the mystery of her voice and vibrational connection to my spirit. This woman's advice somehow penetrated the deepest parts of my mind. Before midnight struck, 11:59, she was sure to hand me a book, *One Flesh*. It's a story about Delilah and how manipulation weakened Samson. I never read the book, but the Cover Label continued to play out in my mind. The devil is a manipulator and seeks to destroy God's anointed, His Son. It's unfortunate that for so long, I put it on the shelf. I gave up my strength when I felt weak because I doubted God's love, the One who put strength within me to just say 'NO' to worldly or fleshly satisfactions.' Sound familiar? I needed God's love, but I traded it for a lie. Why would I believe the lie that I needed love outside of God? I was looking for wholeness in marriage like two becoming one. Wholeness is not like that. You must be whole first, or you will have issues. This explains why many families have issues since we are all in the process of becoming whole and righteous. I was not a good witness for Jesus because I operated in pride and unbelief. In my early adult life, I leaned on my own reasoning, thinking money and titles meant salvation for me. Bobby's father expected us to go to his church, which we did reluctantly and double-mindedly. I suppose some seeds of God's Word were indirectly planted into my young mind. His Christian mother was full of unconditional love, which we all need more of! His mother always spoke about pleasing God, and her favorite scripture passage to quote to us in our teenage rebellion was from Galatians 6:7-8, "You reap what you sow!"

I graduated high school and went to Young Harris College (YHC). Mom wanted me to go to a four-year college, but I thought that her recommendation for me was too much of a party school. Unfortunately, I found myself even deeper into the pit of personal shame because of some lustful relationships and party atmospheres. I wasn't following Christ until after my first year at YHC, but even then, I was just a baby Christian. I wanted to join the churchy sorority, but for whatever reason, I ended up joining the opposite sorority due to majority rule in my dorm complex. In the fall, I joined Phi Delta sorority, and I received my jersey number 34, representing my line of big sisters. I carried a 4.0 GPA in my first quarter but dropped it down to a 2.3 GPA by the end of the second quarter when I joined that sorority. Yikes! I felt like a victim of my choices. I wanted to be victorious, but I embraced the disguise, aka the label, the band-aid of shame. My college days flew by but with lots of confusion. Some people would say I gave the devil a foothold or opened the door to sin. At Young Harris College, I learned a lot about my mixed-up self! Bobby visited my dorm room often, and sometimes, he'd disguise himself under my bed comforter, hoping not to get me in trouble with the resident assistant. At YHC, I made many immature decisions, but I believe God was working through it all to teach me that He was in everything. I liked the sorority I joined, even though I blamed myself for this choice that ruined my mindset for success. They had a turtle mascot, a cross and crescent symbol, and the motto

'Unity through Diversity.' This resonated with me. I was symbolically, at times, like a turtle: fearful, hard to understand, and slow to learn. Diversity also explained who I was. I liked everyone and wanted everyone to like me. This is dangerous because it makes people-pleasing attractive. Who taught us 'people pleasing is important'? As the country singer Waylon Jennings sang, 'Looking for love in all the wrong places.' I loved attention, and this often hurt my relationship with God because the focus was on others' approval. Before I graduated, I did begin to understand God's grace to cover my lustful, crazy ways.

The Difference between Lust and Love

Lust is a purely physical attraction, while love is an emotional bond. It's not uncommon to experience a strong connection with someone attractive right after meeting them, but it's important to differentiate between lust and love. I believe the relationship between Delilah and Samson was lust. This kind is usually based on external factors, such as appearance and connections to power or influence. It is usually selfish love. Lust is sometimes viewed as an immediate feeling that arises upon first encountering someone without the need for time and reflection. However, this first perception can lead to confusion. Love develops over time. It goes past the first impressions through reflection and growth. Understanding romantic relationships is like understanding Chinese or Sanskrit, and it takes a lifetime! It's important to consider the long-term consequences of a relationship that is solely based on lust. Neither Bobby nor I knew the difference between lust and love because we were both from dysfunctional homes. Thinking before you touch or see (as in pornography) can save a relationship from emotional damage. People often mix up lust and love because they can elicit similar feelings, but they are fundamentally different. Some may even confuse lust for love or vice versa. The best way to determine if your feelings are lust or love is to examine their origin. Sometimes, love is blind!

Lust is often characterized by a preoccupation with sexual thoughts and desires when thinking about someone. I knew how to satisfy my boyfriend's desires, which were sexual at the time. My performance or art of teasing this man was my focus. If these thoughts are the primary focus, it may be worth reevaluating the relationship as it may be centered solely on physical pleasure. Lust can be an all-consuming feeling, clouding judgement and leading to impulsive behavior in pursuit of satisfying a physical desire. Consider your ways and recognize the harmful consequences that lust can have, particularly in the form of addiction to pornography. This type of addiction can erode relationships, cause shame, and lead to decreased self-worth. As a result, individuals who struggle with pornography addiction may isolate themselves, perpetuating the issue. Although pornography may appear to satisfy physical desires, it interferes with sexual intimacy and creates a barrier in authentic relationships.

Trauma from trapped emotions and verbal accusations made me angry. Ignoring these toxic relationship issues will only continue the cycle of emotional abuse. I thought condemnation was confirmation of humility in Christ. I did not practice self-respect. I wanted to be accepted, not rejected. I didn't know God's true love. Value and identity are lost when we trade truth for lies. If you think you are in love with the person on a screen, think again: that's not a romantic relationship! We see the illusion of human satisfaction demonstrated in commercials and movies, so we try to repeat it in the bedroom, thinking it will satisfy us, but it never does. The next high or experience just creates more distance from the inner peace we could experience through Jesus Christ.

Additionally, indulging in lustful behaviors, such as excessive spending or ignoring personal responsibilities, can have further negative impacts. If you say, 'I'm addicted to (name),' then you will confirm its existence and validate it. Avoid claiming an addiction to anything. Rather, claim your deliverance from the thing that has pulled you away from God and your inner peace. Once you acknowledge your disobedience to God's way, turn away (repent). Understanding the negative effects of lust or any other addiction upon one's relationships is crucial for personal growth and healing.

The Second Accident

Halloween night changed us. On the night of Bobby's accident, which was the night the Braves won the 1995 World Series, he was dressed up as the commercial Budweiser Woman, and I was disguised as a black cat. I was still a college student, underage for drinking, I may add! We stole beer from the store we worked at so we could party with Bobby's friends. After several drinks and common conversations, he and I argued outside on 10/31/95 for about 45 minutes. I left with his best friend, the faithfully designated driver. Later that evening, my mom received a call from the hospital. Bobby had been in a tragic car wreck. He was rushed to the trauma center. I would've been seated in his Thunderbird had I not left the party after our argument. At that time, I did not know God had spared my life again! That night, I had drunk too much alcohol; I was just a kitten, really. I was confused because when I left the party, I checked his pockets. He didn't have keys! How did he get the keys? He was always thinking ahead! When the DD was headed back to the party, he found Bobby's car flipped upside down on the side of the road. If the female witness, his angel, had not stood beside him while waiting for the ambulance, I'm sure he would not have survived. The wreck was so tragic! Supposedly, the man driving the van that crashed into him, after running through a red light, was delivering speakers to a church at one o'clock in the morning! This witness prayed for him until he was transported to the trauma center. Just an hour before the wreck, we were ending our relationship due to jealousy and the judgements toward one another while intoxicated. After the emergency notification call, Mom dropped me off at the hospital to see Bobby, and the hospital staff questioned my ability to reason. The medical staff believed Bobby would not survive and suggested we pay our respects. They said he'd be lucky if he lived, and they sent us all to the hospital Chaplin. The following week, his father was asked to meet an officer at the junkyard to view the Thunderbird. The police officer asked his father to place his hand on the vehicle because he believed it was truly a miracle his son survived. His dad turned white, realizing it was a miracle God spared his only son. This event was unexplainable! A mystery, for sure! Bobby had a call on his life, too! Two weeks later, he was released to recover at home. He lost five teeth and punctured a lung. The laceration across his cheek is a kind reminder of God's grace. Bobby started to listen closely to the voice of God after his accident. The mystery of my relationship with Bobby continued even past October 31st, 1995, the night I could have lost my life due to the impact on the car, I would have been in.

Bobby and I were almost two years into our relationship. Like a magnet, I stayed with him as he promised to never drink again. Labeled as a black cat, the girlfriend, who could not make up her mind, decided to love and forgive. Were our Halloween costumes an identity coverup? Maybe the miraculous clues from the car accidents were leading us toward God. I knew a shift was happening back then, even though it took years to manifest. I believe in the supernatural divine power of God that chose this family for me and which I was destined to mix blood with. Matthew 19:6 and Mark 10:9 NIV state, "...what God has joined together, let no one separate.". We didn't need a marriage document because we were already joined together as one flesh, in a sense. Shame can potentially haunt you like a shadow all your life if you don't bring it to the Son of the Living God, exposing shame. A wise family member quoted, "Your reputation is like a shadow. It follows you everywhere you go." We do need to be careful how we live because emotions lodge in the body and cause lots of pain. The emotional attachment to Bobby became my reputation, lasting into my forties. I struggled to release my feelings, and therefore, I was mentally bound to the idea that I had to perform to be loved!

Bobby and I started attending a spirit-filled church in 1995 after the accident. This church hosted their very first Heart to Heart Women's Conference in 1996. At that event, the seed for this book was planted in my heart. When someone is called to write a book, it may take many years to develop the content. God equips teachers, preachers, evangelists, prophets, and workers of miracles through life trials. This calling was before I had any clue about being spirit-filled.

Just one semester before graduating college, a strange

phenomenon happened. Bobby and I had an angel experience! One winter evening, before a sorority rush event for the rising freshmen, Bobby and I were traveling from the college in search of a secluded campsite. We drove up a mountain about two miles to a dead end within a state park. It was getting late; the sun was setting, and I had to get back to college. We had walked away from his new Ford Ranger truck (since he crashed the Thunderbird) looking for the perfect campsite, but unknowingly, a mountain lion or some kind of panther was pursuing us. We heard some crackling and growling just off the distance, but the dusk kept us from spotting it. We raced back to the Ford Ranger truck, and to our surprise, we were delayed by a flat tire.

"Oh no! What happened!" I frantically cried.

"It's no problem, don't worry, I know how to change a tire!" Bobby confidently replied.

Bobby knew a lot about Ford vehicles since that is all his dad worked on, but strangely, maybe for a supernatural reason, he could not find where the jack was! All I knew to do was pray for help. It was getting dark, and we didn't have a flashlight. Literally, out of nowhere came a white police car and two very tall men, one white and one African American. They stepped out of the car and asked how they could help. Within what seemed like a couple of minutes, they had the jack and the spare tire and had finished changing the tire. Neither Bobby nor I even remember their faces. Bobby and I started to descend the hill in his new vehicle and headed back to the school in the dark.

"Wait! Stop! That was so weird. Do you hear or see anything?" I asked Bobby.

We waited quietly at the bottom of the hill with our lights off and for over five minutes, not a sound or light was seen. Surely, we would have heard something or seen headlights from their vehicle on that winter evening! Nothing! I thought that was extremely strange. There was nowhere for them to go because we were already at the top, and it was a dead end at the top of the mountain. We questioned, 'Why was a regular police car going to the place we were anyways? Were they angels?' Bobby and I were dumbfounded! It had to have been an experience with angels! Another miracle! It was a crazy experience, but it was real to us.

I knew I needed to graduate college, so I worked hard to increase my GPA. I graduated with an Associate of Science from YHC. I wanted to finish a bachelor's degree, but that would mean relocating and applying for more financial aid. YHC was doing a Spring Alumni Giving event. I just happened to be assigned to call alumni. One of the alumni, who did not want to give to the college, found out what sorority I was part of, and she wanted to send me on a free trip to New York with my boyfriend to visit her city. She also donated money specifically for me to finish YHC! God was making a way for my blessing to come!

Before graduating, we partnered with a multi-level marketing company, Amway and the Bill Britt organization. We met some amazing people who led us spiritually. I felt alive and prosperous, with hope for my future! Was this predestined, a distraction of the enemy, or our choice? I will forever be grateful for this detour because of some amazing leadership, memories, and trips. We still have many leadership books for training. We went to lots of business and spiritual training meetings, some that started at 9 pm at Steak and Shake

Diner. We traveled to late-night meetings in our leader's house each week. I grew exponentially in my faith and would even share the gospel with almost every new person I met. I can remember sharing the gospel with people on buses, airplanes, and in Walmart. We learned a lot of life principles to live by. I remember Bill saying at a conference, 'If I lost all this (pointing to the thousands of people who helped him grow his wealth), I could get it all back because I know the one who gave it to me.' He was a Christian, our leaders were Christian, and God needed us to learn from them. Bobby proposed to me at an Amway meeting. I said Yes without hesitation. I knew he loved me, and that was all I thought I needed to become who I wanted to be.

Love and new beginnings excited me, and so I decided Mom needed someone, too! One evening, I was out prospecting alone for Amway customers at Walmart! Yes, I did say Walmart! I met a handsome veteran. This man was soon to become my mom's boyfriend. I asked Mom to at least meet him one time, and reluctantly, she met him at Waffle House. Before mom spoke to him, she knew she was hooked because when he stepped out of his Tahoe, she noticed he had legs she would think about all night! We still talk about that day!

God is always working to bless us, even when we think what we are going through is an attack or a sign that he is not working for our benefit. When Bobby and I asked the church staff secretary about getting married in the church, we learned some unfortunate news. That pastor had some family issues to work on, so the next in line was someone that only God would choose, a spiritually innocent African American, to do our wedding! Later, we learned that he had an admiration for

Bobby's sister, who was working in the baby ministry. Bobby and I were satisfied with anyone ordained to do the job, but we did not know that this man would cause a stumbling block that would divide Bobby's sister and their dad. She was kicked out of the house for her rebellion. Religion can be a good thing, but it can also be an idol or a cult, dividing families. Throwing out the baby with the bath water is what happened. There comes a point in life when who you are on the inside comes to the surface. If you want a clear consciousness, the trash inside us must be taken out. It's uncomfortable when the inside comes out and clashes with what is presented on the outside. The fruit on the tree will be known. As a deacon of a church, his dad had to release his racist beliefs. The pride band-aid had to come off! Thank God we no longer have that issue, because God did the miraculous work in his heart over many years. Bobby's sister and our wedding minister later married and had four boys. The secret to true love lies in the power of revealing the deep issue that keeps you separated from your healing. "Therefore, confess your sins to each other so that you may be healed."[7] Secrets are just like band-aids covering scars. When they are uncovered, someone always gets hurt but the longer it stays covered, the more it becomes infected. It's good practice to keep the identity label transparent! I'm so thankful my sister-in-law's husband is a man of righteousness, a believer. Many are called, but few will listen and walk in the way that leads to life.

The year Bobby and I were married, my first cousin was battling a rare, aggressive cancer. At our church, miracles were common. I felt that the faith-filled believers who attended

---

[7] James 5:16

regularly had a connection with God that could shift the direction of the winds and uproot trees deep in the ocean. I took my request to them, but my cousin lived in another state; therefore, he could not come to our church. We decided that the ladies would lay hands on me as the conduit for God to perform supernatural healing in his body. It was a very emotional and powerful experience. Some people would label this type of belief as a miracle in favor of the impossible. After the prayer, we had him go to the doctor and the cancer was gone! Yes, his faith in God healed him! Who would've thought that the cancer could be eradicated through intercessory prayer! "The prayer of a righteous person is powerful and effective."[8] I was not righteous by my life disciplines, but I was made righteous by my faith in Jesus, who knew no sin. The doctors, who probably didn't believe in God, recommended he continue chemo just to make sure he was indeed cancer-free. He did not make it to our wedding in 1997 because the continued Chemo treatment was too hard on his already frail body, and he possibly lost his desire to press on. This was super hard emotionally because I felt like my cousin gave up too easily, but I can't even imagine the pain he experienced. I thought God had turned his back on my cousin and his new family. Everything was going so well! He was able to come to Georgia for my sister's wedding in May of the same year we married.

Often, when emotions go haywire, our brains fog. Just five months before our wedding, my thoughts and emotions were in disarray, which was a perfect opportunity for deception to enter. I remember leaving work and trying to process my life.

---

[8] James 5:16

I had a one-night stand with a co-worker from the restaurant I worked at. I was supposed to be a born-again good Christian, plus I was engaged! I felt so guilty and full of shame! I held this shameful secret for years before confessing to my spouse. Neither of us were pure in our sexual actions, and God knew this, but we thought we could hide.

One year after our wedding, we moved from our apartment, which was close to all city conveniences, into a starter home in the north rural area. Our distance from most of Bobby's family and being the new woman in the family (a wife) created some conflict. My mind was not stable with a peaceful confidence from the Lord. I feared judgment since we were leaders at our church. Jesus knew we would be persecuted and rejected, but we would be protected, spared, and saved from death. An Amway leadership book helped me gain wisdom, "Battlefield of the Mind" by Joyce Meyer. It changed my life! I was a lot like this woman, confused by sexual interpretations. She inspired me to overcome my battle within! Distance can create issues in relationships. I was working as a server, and Bobby was working at a grocery store. His family expressed some bitterness toward us not being available, but the city life was not our preference. The starter home we chose was about half an hour from our church. This house already had one room with a baby design, but I didn't think much about it. The financial stress started to wedge into our relationship. I wasn't sure if Bobby could love me because I didn't finish a bachelor's degree. My unbelief became my thorn in my flesh, like Paul in the bible. I had some unhealthy outcome agreements in my head that grew into python-sized eggs. When a person has python eggs in their head, as Jentezen Franklin, the pastor of Free Chapel in

Gainesville, GA preached, the thoughts they produce can destroy your whole life if you let it. I made myself a victim without power to overcome. I was sick, not physically, just emotionally. I owed a debt for my sin (unbelief) because I could not understand that the way to success could come by grace, not just works. Just like Rome, it was taxes, slavery, unemployment, and diseases that contributed to the fall. Band-aids of shame from college cultural choices, bad habits, premarital sex, and fear of acceptance kept me from believing in supernatural possibilities. I questioned if God was for me, not against me. Did God still destine Bobby and me to help each other grow closer to Him? What was love anyways? Both of our families had experienced unfortunate relationships and broken hearts, but I felt like God was sending me the message that this man was part of my destiny.

Just a few weeks into our new home, I found out I was pregnant, which was not by surprise since we had been talking about children; however, I was afraid of the remnant of experimental drugs from my wild party life in college that could affect the child. I knew God was up to something big in this faith test. When we went to the OB/GYN to find the sex of the child, the doctors recommended an amniocentesis to clarify their concerns about the baby's brain. We had to go downtown to a specialist. We were really seeking the Lord and growing in faith, but we decided to make the appointment to have the amniocentesis procedure. We agreed in faith that the doctors would find nothing concerning, the baby would flip in the womb, and I would deliver a healthy baby. That band-aid of fear was ripped off before we knew the results! I was in a personal spiritual revival. I believe that our experience with our Amway leadership had much to do with our mental training for such a time. We believed I would have a supernatural delivery as well. We had faith that she was perfect and that the doctors would confirm this agreement. "All looks good, and she is perfect!" We declared favor because we knew we were blessed. Anytime we agree with faith, not fear, miracles take root, and the devil's assignment is cancelled! I believe that each child is a gift from heaven above, and that is why the devil wants to corrupt the seed (the thoughts and perspectives) as soon as possible. As parents, we did not allow the seed of fear to take root, although the pregnancy was painful, uncomfortable, and questionable. We knew that standing firm on truth, the living and active sword of the Word of God, would confirm the gift we were given by His amazing grace! My delivery was fast and not painful at all. It was almost supernatural! For three years and beyond, she was the center of everything, bringing joy into many lives, until she was joined by her brother, who would bring a bright light to the world too.

I joined a small local ladies' gym to lose the twenty-five extra pounds I gained. I also became an aerobics instructor. I was a terrible instructor at first, but Bobby patiently endured being my guinea pig student. It was a fun challenge because he had no rhythm or coordination. He was so funny. He loved me in a way I struggled to comprehend because I doubted my ability. This struggle is common, and we often do not see how God is equipping us. Bobby loved me so much that he would get frustrated or upset with me because I did not believe in myself. When two people are chosen, united, and of the same vibrational energy, there is positive power. Bobby's mother's spiritual influence was passed onto Bobby. I can remember Bobby praying in tongues of fire around our apartment, our starter home, and our current home. Just because someone is spirit-filled, this does not mean they never sin! No one is perfect, and God would make sure I did not hold this expectation over anyone who I thought was a Christian. God would not allow me to get too big for my britches because pride does go before the fall. God was sending us signs and miracles as part of our story together, but we were still asleep spiritually and covering ourselves with Band-aids because they felt comfortable and familiar. We still believed we had to earn our salvation by paying penance to the church for our sins. Pleasing the ego (my flesh) as a wounded soldier from my worldview crisis resulted in a trivial life to piece together. When I was working at the lady's gym, growing my Amway business, and ministering to people about Jesus, I remember how the Spirit would move, and I would speak in tongues while in prayer over people I encountered. After four years of 'chasing the get-rich-quick carrot,' we stopped our Amway business since it was harder to travel with a baby girl.

    I also remember a day when Bobby was headed home from work, and he found a beautiful wildflower between rocks at the railroad crossing. He brought it to me and told me it was special and beautiful, just like me. He didn't know then how this spoke to me. I was just like that flower, Wild between the rocks. The rocks were Jesus and Man. Only one rock can satisfy. When a flower is found between rocks, it's like the flower is crying out to be noticed. I felt like my flesh was crying, but my Spirit was not loosening. It felt paralyzed. This story reminds me of the verse, "I tell you, … if they keep quiet, the stones will cry out."[9] Sometimes, we all struggle to

---

[9] Luke 19:40

communicate for fear that we will be rejected. We had trouble in our relationship because we could not successfully communicate the thoughts we dealt with and empathize or understand each other's perspectives. I had a friend from church who I would verbally sort out all my marriage issues with because I felt like she understood me. We were actively serving in the youth program my brother-in-law started called About Face. This program helped lead the youth into an About Face, a 180-degree turn toward God. A misdirected lifestyle needs hope of redemption. My husband and I were perfect examples of rebellious kids in need of hope. This program was amazingly effective among teens and adults. We enjoyed ministry trips in Gatlinburg, TN, where teens witnessed the effect of fervent prayer. These were the golden years for us. Our spiritual growth in ministry and the many miraculous salvations among the youth gave us a foundation for service in other churches. I was also part of the street ministry in downtown Atlanta with a warrior African American female deliverance minister. When two or more agree in prayer, manifestations of the Holy Spirit happen, such as a person going from panic and fight to a calm and peaceful state of mind. Many times, she would lay hands on the mentally imbalanced and experience their demonic deliverance on site. It was a crazy experience, but it was real! I could relate witnessing to the mentally imbalanced because I had a cousin who was a crazy alcoholic.

Numbers Matter

Have you ever feared the meaning of a number? Look at the biblical account in Genesis 11 about the Tower of Babel. The number eleven represents destruction. Before 9/11 happened, I Became a distributor for AdvoCare, a multi-vitamin company just before my son was born. Something inside began to fear that things were changing. I used to see the number eleven everywhere. Even my aunt in Texas claimed the same phenomenon. My AdvoCare business was bringing in a minimal to moderate side income until a few years later when they changed the supplement formulas. After one of my aerobics classes, I was having an AdvoCare mixer at my house. However, that morning changed everything in the world as we knew it. It was 9/11/01. I've always been interested in numbers and how they play into the events of our lives – often, they can be quite mysterious. Many of us take numbers for granted without realizing that different societies interpret numbers based on their customs and beliefs. There are some numbers that carry a lot of spiritual weight, and understanding their meaning can help us see how they influence different cultures physically. It's fascinating to me how such a small concept can have such a big impact on our world. Considering the 9-11 attacks, I was reminded that even though the number eleven may have negative connotations for some, it can also represent miracles and protection. The fact that many people were miraculously not in the buildings during the attacks showed the power of divine intervention. Additionally, the two towers that were hit by Flight 11 could also be interpreted as a representation of the number eleven.

We asked the Lord for a son. The Lord is always directing our steps even when we think we are in control. Bobby and I believed that if we followed all the recommendations for having a boy, we could create one as if we could mechanically do it. Ha-ha! On a gut whim, I changed gyms just before the ladies' gym closed, and I miraculously got hired at the YMCA without knowing I was pregnant with my second child. I remember the day I went into labor with our son; I was teaching a kickboxing class at the YMCA. No, my water did not break while teaching, but it was quite entertaining to see the crowds of members staring at my very large pregnant belly bouncing around while instructing high-intensity kickboxing and step aerobics classes. That evening I went into labor, and we went to eat wings at Buffalos. I may have eaten about 25 scorchin' hot wings on my own. We went to the hospital, they broke my water, and nothing happened. I walked the halls and could have done some skipping, but still no baby. The pregnancy with him was super easy. I barely felt pregnant, but the delivery was confirmation that I was done having kids. He was a miracle baby, too, because the umbilical cord had a knot in it, and I almost had to have a C-section because his oxygen was down. The doctor stated, 'Had I not been in such good shape, we could have lost the baby.' I knew Bobby would need to get himself fixed so we couldn't have any more kids. Originally, I thought I wanted six kids, but after two deliveries, I was determined not to go through the pain of childbirth again.

    I started a fine dining server job in the evenings at the mall. There was a friendly co-worker who made fun of me for having to pump breast milk in the middle of the dinner shift for my son. Bobby would come home from his grocery store job, and I would go serve tables. The money was helpful, but our relationship was suffering. Our marriage, like many marriages, had two broken people living in a fallen world. Even though I was struggling with trust, I still heard from the Lord. One day I went to work at the mall and felt the Spirit of God tell me to quit. A week later, my boss called me and told me she could not get into the restaurant, yet she had the keys.

I was sad for her. Fortunately, I still had a job as an aerobics instructor. I was beginning to hear from God more, but I did not fully trust Him at the time.

There were two fear words that I allowed in my mind: distance and divorce. I believed lies and feared the common paradigms of unfaithfulness and abandonment that sometimes happen in marriages. When our thoughts go haywire, they are like a python gripping our ability to live well! This fear mentality hurt my relationship with Bobby. Was it related to the root of rejection? Most likely, a psychiatrist could label and prescribe medication for the anxiety I felt. I was raising two young kids, helping my husband with meals, bills, and laundry, as well as working part-time. This was not how I thought I would spend my days. Some women dream of this, but I wanted to be able to support myself just in case I ended up single and struggling like my mom. Security is a big issue for most women, whether it is the security of relationships, finances, or true love. What do we love more? That's where our security lay. I did my best to plug into a church and study God's word, but I struggled to trust God would provide. It's important to ask yourself, 'What are my beliefs?' Am I believing what I see or what I do not see?

After 9/11, I began reflecting again on the number 11 and it's meaning in a more positive perspective. I started on a journey to know God again. I had slipped away a little. I was reminded that the story of salvation and hope embodied in the birth of Jesus can offer comfort and reassurance, even in the face of tragedy and destruction. Our nation united to save people from the flames. I wonder if more people think about hell as eternity or hell on earth. What was meant for bad had some positive turnout because people started loving and serving again. Hebrews 11 became my favorite verse during this time. I started looking up a lot of scripture verses with this number. The Story of Jesus' birth is referenced in Luke 2:11 NIV, "Today in the town of David a Savior has been born to you; he is the Messiah, the Lord." In Matthew 2:11 NIV, the scripture references the Magi who followed a star to the place of the Savior to worship him. These verses gave me comfort that the number eleven did not have to relate to destruction. "In God, I trust and am not afraid. What can man do to me?"[10] "I am the resurrection and the life. The one who believes in me will live, even though they die…"[11] When we find our identity in Christ, we are able to see ourselves through His eyes, and that allows us to believe the things He says about us. His opinion is the only one that matters, and it can be the one that we constantly seek. Our identity issues can only be fixed by God. He is the only one who knows who we truly are and what we can achieve if we let Him live in our lives. *"I will be with you"*[12] tells us that God is always with us through every problem and circumstance. He is there with resources to offer us if we let Him. However, too often, we cling to fear and miss the opportunities we could have received if we had just believed. God knows we will experience fear. He doesn't want us to stay there because fear and paralysis go hand in hand. That's why he said over 365 times, "Do not fear!"

I wanted to make right what was a major issue in my marriage: money topics. At the time, the program would be three more years of school, but I had two kids! I had the

---

[10] Psalm 56:11

[11] John 11:25

[12] Exodus 3:12 NIV

perspective that communication would be better between Bobby and me if I had just focused on a career that could fix our stress. I applied and prepared all the documents to attend North Georgia College, but Bobby shared his thoughts that it was not good timing since we had young kids. The world's message of mediocrity became an angry stronghold within me. This caused me to hold bitterness toward myself for not finishing school, and I blamed Bobby for holding me back. It was not him! I held myself back. I let fear of school loans, time commitment, years passing, and the fear of a loss of connection with my kids keep me idle, and I did not take ownership of my own decision to believe that I could go back to college. I was smart and intuitive, but I was also spiritually blind for a period. I did lots of multi-level marketing jobs, which also included liquid supplements and Mary Kay makeup. We won a trip to Cancun, Mexico, with the Biometics company! That was awesome! I was always willing to try but did not seem to make much money because I would get discouraged when Bobby withdrew from the company we were working together. He was all in at the beginning, with great support.

Our starter home didn't have much of a backyard. My husband trusted in the Lord to provide a new house for us. It was time to move. We needed more space with two kids and homeschooling. Bobby found a three-acre lot in a neighborhood about five miles away. The day he took me to the property, it was rainy and cold. The house was rented, and they didn't clean up anything. I was thinking, 'Not gonna' happen!' Well, he walked me back to the end of the 3-acre property and said, 'Turn around and look!' When I saw the massive storybook old Oak tree, I knew it was a no-brainer, we must have it! Bobby said, "Trust me!" I did, and we put our first house in the listings to sell. And before we had the sign in the yard, we had two offers! Within thirty days, we moved! That is Godspeed. During that time, a Spirit of hope was birthed again. Both Bobby and I had just finished Bible College at Tabernacle International Church (TIC), and it helped us lay better foundations. Not a foothold of fear at the time, just the best of the best! I truly felt the unstoppable power of the Holy Spirit because of the miracles! The experience encouraged my faith.

After about one year of nagging my husband about my Nanny living alone, we built an addition to our new home and moved my grandmother in with us. My son was about six years old at that time. I knew it was going to bless her and our family. Rather than her moving to a nursing home after my grandfather passed away or moving to Texas or to North GA, it was just best for her to remain in the same town she was used to. My husband sacrificed his peace for our pleasure. We started building onto our house and counted this project as part of the kids' school day. It was so cool to watch the construction of another little house added to our house! We kept homeschooling and taking karate lessons. We had the good 'ole days with Hallmark movies, and family dinners, fresh sourdough cinnamon bread each week, and lots of funny stories about Nanny. She loved our first family dog, Jonah. I remember laughing so hard because she was calling my son's name while staring at the dog on the other side of the glass back door, asking him what he wanted because he was playfully barking at her. She was such a hoot! When he got sick, I think my husband took it hard. From that day forward, he had a hard time dealing with death. He would suppress all his emotions. Although Bobby's comfort and desires for intimacy were challenged, my Nanny was a blessing to all of us as we endured the busy life of school, karate, and work. Her funny ways, her special cooking, and her Hallmark entertainment still make me smile! My Nanny was known as the sourdough bread lady at her church because she brought four loaves of cinnamon sourdough bread every Sunday to give away. Though she went to a traditional Baptist church, the people there were not too religious. They were genuine, faithful followers of Christ. If it wasn't for my grandmother's prayers, I could have completely lost my mind, because I was too busy! Business is the devil's playground. I've always managed to do an entire day of work before noon or at least by 3 pm, and I could whip up a healthy dinner in 15 minutes. Nanny never understood that because she was old school, meaning you didn't cook unless you were in the kitchen for over an hour per square meal. Her meals included starch vegetables and some kind of floured and fried meat. Bobby loved her cooking. If I didn't tell her what to cook, we'd have fried chicken legs and thighs with canned green beans scorched to the pan. It was good and full of flavor! She didn't mind cooking, but I did most of the cooking. She watched the kids so Bobby and I could go out on dates, and she helped with laundry and meals. Our kids learned so much from her, including history about the good 'ole days after the Depression, how to iron and sew, make biscuits, and communicate in prayer to God. Often, on our way home, she would have our usual healthy meal of tilapia and zucchini squash! I never made the same meal twice, so she'd always say, 'Are we going to have this again, or do you want me to write down the recipe?' She loved helping us, but it was important that she felt appreciated. I believe we helped her enjoy life and feel young again. I made her exercise with weights and eat healthy meals. My grandmother was always so thankful and joyful. I remember her opening her door that opened into our kitchen and her first words, 'Good morning, Beautiful!' She was always fully dressed and ready to be a blessing! I'm sure our kids learned a lot about love and respect from her. She was a model of good spirits! If it wasn't for her love, I could've lost all hope under the pressure of a changing economy and the tensions between Bobby and me.

Chapter Three
Training

"Unless there is ownership for your decisions, there will be no discipline, and no understanding of the choices, and therefore no true freedom."

–Classical Conversations

If God equips the called, you can be confident he will train you until you know you are competent and ready for the next level. His grace is allowing you to keep taking the test until you pass it. I'm not talking about taking a hall pass or a get-out-of-jail pass, and I'm talking about finishing the race. When the author of the book is finished, he feels peace. God is the Alpha and the Omega, the Beginning and the End.[13] Trusting the Creator is like being in the flow. Imagine young kids playing while they discover the playground or a video game. It could be fun! Think about life like a Pac-Man game! You may have some ghosts you have to go through. I heard a quote, but I'm not sure who said it, "New levels, new devils." We could praise God when we make it to a new level because we get new opportunities to pass that level, too! There is a reward, even if it is only points on a screen. See how looking at it differently moves you through it? Some levels take us longer to conquer, but the goal is to conquer and overcome the enemy. Not to quit! Many times, in my life, I wanted to quit because I did not have faith either in myself, my situation, or someone else. We must let go of our own understanding and let God do the miraculous! That's what God is a master at! He

---
[13] Revelation 22:13 NIV

has had lots of practice. I'm sure some of us feel like we are a little Extra! I did. I can hear the tabloid headline, "Extra, Extra, read all about her!" We never want to read the boring stuff, the self-help books, or the directions to a new piece of equipment. We want to read the gossip! As a homeschool mom, I was always reading self-help material on how to keep a Christian home and raise kids ready for the world. A family friend gave us a book about building family values. We made a family shield with four visions: Confidence, Teamwork, Respect, and Family. These visions were not clear realities from the experiences which Bobby and I had in our childhood. There were times I wanted to throw out the family shield because I felt like we would never get there.

When my daughter was about four years old, a very close family friend gave me a gift with this prayer, "Build me a daughter, O Lord, who will be strong enough to know her own strengths, self-confident enough to face the challenges of today and tomorrow, one who will accept defeat with determination, success with grace and wisdom." Confidence cannot be trained like a skill that builds one's competence. In the world's eyes, a confident person is evident by their competence. If competence precedes confidence, then we will always feel like we need to keep learning before we ever act. I see this all the time. We won't even go to church because we are not doing enough right to deserve to sit in church. We've lost our confidence that God could "love a wretch like me." We think our practices must be perfect before we share our faith. "Now faith is confidence in what we hope for and assurance about what we do not see."[14] You cannot see

---

[14] Hebrews 11:1 KJV

confidence, but you know it when you see it in a person, and believe me, that takes time to develop. My daughter is now a Registered Nurse. She is richly confident in God, and she understands the power of words. When she writes her vision, speaks her vision, and believes the Almighty God to perform it, she could almost be afraid to ask because it most likely comes true. I've always told her she is blessed and highly favored. She does not walk in fear. I'm so proud of our daughter! She is a natural leader. As her primary teacher, I trained her, but ultimately, God is her teacher!

God will test our faith. In the bible, Abraham's faith was tested on Mt. Moriah. Faith is the most important test we'll ever have to take. God is the only one who knows our hearts, and he knows his people! He raises us up from ground zero. Unfortunately, that means unlearning your own methods. Proverbs 14:12 states, "There is a way that seems right unto man, but in the end, it leads to death." We cannot win the battle fighting with human reason. Start cutting down the pride that rears its egoic head. Matthew 3:10 states, "The ax is already at the root of the trees, and every tree that does not produce good fruit will be cut down and thrown into the fire." Faith in leadership takes time to develop. Even Moses doubted his ability to lead the Israelites. He is quoted saying, "I AM who I AM." It's through life experiences that we find out what we don't want and what we do want. I wanted those four family core values. Confidence comes from the Lord; competence comes from the world. When we put all our trust in the Lord, he gives us the confidence to keep training! I learned from spiritual teachers who had experience following the world and following the Lord. Our training from the Lord is never an easy road. God connected me to the best people on earth for training in righteousness through Amway leaders, The Tabernacle International, the homeschool groups, and great lifelong friends. A Christian is not a Christian because they have learned overnight how to be perfect. Accepting ourselves and finding contentment along the journey could give us more peace. If you seek peace, you will find it. Peace is a great gift when you don't know what direction the Lord is leading you to travel. Look for inner peace, and you'll know the Way.

Listening to the Spirit is part of the training. When God called me to homeschool, I later found out that my local rural church had a group of women who homeschooled, and they had mom's night out meetings. The first meeting I went to, I was almost ready to back out because I labeled myself different from them. They were qualified and very much perfect with all their kids and books! I didn't even like to read! Being a social parent, I decided to join the homeschool group and attend some homeschool conventions. I met some amazing people! I remember attending an evening "mom's night out" event at one of the mom's houses when the Holy Spirit specifically told me to pray for one of the other moms. Everyone was leaving, and my emotions and heart were jumping. Just before this lady left, I stopped her and asked if I could pray for her. She came back into the house. I laid hands on her, along with the other moms, and began to pray. The Spirit was so intense I began to pray in tongues. I don't even know what I said. The next day, she called the host's mom and claimed she had no pain and slept through the night! All I can say is obedience is always better than following fear of what people will think of you.

Your Position Matters

Archimedes quoted, "Give me a lever long enough and a fulcrum on which to place it, and I shall move the world." When our kids were young, we did Tang Soo Do karate for about 10 ½ years. Our instructor stated, 'Your position matters.' This stuck with me because I had been in the wrong position spiritually. I was not meant to be the spiritual leader, but I knew the kids needed spiritual training. Symbolically, I took a few knockouts until I learned where to stand. Karate with my kids was better than just watching them. Although karate was not a team sport, I counted it as teamwork because the kids and I would not have been able to take lessons if it wasn't for my husband's financial support and my grandmother making dinner for the family. This contact sport really impacted our lives, not only because of the lessons we learned but it helped us develop confidence. Our commitment to karate helped us gain more competence, too. After about 3 ½ years, the kids and I had black belts! We had another rank to make us feel important and noticed. My son and I continued for another seven years to earn our 3rd-degree black belts. I trained for a year in Brazilian Jujitsu, and my son trained for almost three years.

Ironically, through karate we simultaneously were spiritually trained to quickly notice an attack from our enemy. His attacks are sneaky when we are not alert. If you are ready, you won't get injured because you have been trained to move. If we were in the wrong position, we would be injured. Symbolically, for every rank we tested, if we passed, we would have a ceremony recognizing the old and stepping into the new. We would face our master instructor, turn around, take off our old rank, get on our knees and fold our belt, push it away, stand up, turn, and face our instructor again, and bow, step forward, and then hold out our arms as he tied the next recognizing rank around our waist, then we would bow again. This is a symbolic practice of recognizing your training and humbling yourself for the training in the new rank is like Pac-Man, new levels, new devils. We should never get too big for our britches, just keep learning. There were days in karate when I was so confident with all my spiritual might even my sparring partner would question his own strength. Humble shepherd boy David had faith like a giant, too! I know God positions us for greatness, but for some of us, it takes years of experience to finally be in a position for God to awaken us. It's like an epiphany or Ah-ha moment. Before we are awakened, we only see the back side of the tapestry, the pieces of the threads and the messiness of the backstory. We don't see God protecting us. The kids also took music lessons for seven years from a beautiful family friend who loves the Lord! This was an additional investment! The more you invest, not just in money but also time, the more your return on investment. It may have been more popular to do baseball, football, or cheerleading, but we were homeschoolers, so we already broke the cookie-cutter mold. I had a friend tell me I was not a real homeschooler until I had four years invested. I learned a lot about position and perspective when I stayed with something long enough.

The first ten years of homeschooling were God-inspired, God-directed, and God-ordered. We enjoyed many field trips and random homeschool classes with the Eagles homeschool program, which I helped direct. I met an amazing person in the Eagles program who had two girls. Our kids became best friends. I directed the PE classes and started a branch Eagles homeschool program at my grandmother's church. After a few years, I started a group in my home for some extracurricular activities with other homeschoolers. Field days and PE in our backyard with the two homeschool groups, which I time managed very well, was crazy fun! Having a leadership position in everything I did, whether in a home school group or the church, filled the emptiness of my personal contentment and worldly approval. Still looking for those Band-aids, I continued to find another identity or form of attachment. I grew up in leadership within the homeschool community, but the Lord kept me humble. Change hurts at first, like a Band-aid ripping off, but knowing that ownership leads to discipline, I knew I had to take ownership if I wanted to grow.

A friend from karate introduced me to the Classical Conversations Homeschool Program. I attended a CC Day at the director's house and truly felt God connecting us to these amazing women and their kids. One of the moms had four kids, and the other had six kids at the time. My two were eleven years old and eight years old. We joined Classical Conversations, a homeschool program that gave us another foundation for our faith and identity in Christian communities. This program was the "foundation and village" I heard God tell me before I answered the call to homeschool. The first program in CC was called Foundations. Classical Conversations is a program of three levels called the Trivium: Foundations Grammar, Dialectic, and Rhetoric. The CC mission is 'to know God and make Him known.' One of the directors was quoted stating, 'Children are souls to be nurtured, not products to be measured.' We were beginning the Foundation's program as a confirmation, which God told me about a couple of years prior. The first scriptures in the book of Genesis and John are the foundations! "In the beginning was the Word, and the Word was with God, and the Word was God. He was with God in the beginning."[15] Without foundation, we become confused, and we have the wrong lenses! We have the wrong interpretation of science, and we cannot see the mysteries of God since our ego intercedes our thoughts and separates us from God. Often, in our busy course of life, we lose our foundation, trying to be the savior to others. If one wants to know God, they must not rush through life trying to do everything alone or perfectly, but rather, it is better to do a few things well with the community or your village. At one summer training practicum, the instructor mentioned a scripture about a plumb line in Amos 7:7-8. I felt like I needed a plumb line, a standard for measure, for my family. Ironically, this tool is something my son uses daily in his career. This program helped our kids to train their brains to retain. Not only did they learn study skills that would help them in college and life, but they also memorized a lot of scripture foundational facts and practiced using social skills. They learned debate, logic, Latin, and public speaking. The standard for the measure was spiritual growth and evidence that their souls were nurtured. We did not focus on grading our kids. CC was not concerned about the quantity of work. What mattered was the quality of conversation and relationship. Many great teachers have taught that it is better to do one thing well than do many and get nothing out of it. Our American education is flooded with much to know, yet I would argue that our kids are not smarter. We developed close friendships and grew the foundation of our faith, our village, and our respect for our world. The best part of my day was recessing every Tuesday

---

[15] John 1:1-2

at Classical Conversations when I could talk with my friends and watch the kids play with their friends for 30 minutes. Our CC director was the best! I don't know how she managed to homeschool seven kids and direct our program. My husband trusted me without having to research the program because my peace was evident. I spent lots of money and time in this rigorous program to prepare our kids for the diabolical world, as C.S. Lewis wrote about in Screwtape Letters. It takes a village of people who are sensitive to the Holy Spirit to train up the little ones.

After a couple of years, I was asked to direct the seventh-grade program since my daughter was moving into seventh grade. It was a great opportunity to make more money and have fun with my daughter's peers! We had some fun memories, including the CC Day my kids had their Papa Ronnie as the star! He brought a freshwater fish to fillet and fry for my daughter's seventh-grade class. Memories that will never be forgotten! When I was the Challenge A Director, I had two rules: Listen and Learn and Listen and Obey. I needed to listen twice and learn to obey the first time! As a Challenge director, I taught Latin, which is a subject I cheated in when I was in high school. It's funny how God allowed me to humbly take Latin again as a teacher!

Family is another one of our core values. Homeschooling was great for our family! Even my husband took part in making school memorable or a little less serious. Our son learned a lot of things from his daddy, who loved to have fun pranking people, but it was all fun. Once, my husband put a toad on the counter when I was cooking. When I saw it, I about peed on myself! He laughed so hard! He loved making life fun! One time, as a young teen, our son locked my Nanny in the bathroom as a joke because the lock had been installed backwards. A few minutes later, my landline phone on our side of the house rang. It was my grandmother! Fortunately, she carried her house phone everywhere, otherwise we would never have heard her yelling for someone to come let her out of her own bathroom. He was always playing pranks on her. It was kind of funny! I remember my grandmother's claims about our son, "How can you be so good-looking and be so aggravating at the same time?" He probably learned how to not take life so seriously from his daddy. Our kids enjoyed other life skills, too, including outdoor adventures such as homeschool family camping trips and field days with friends. Bobby trained our son to deer hunt, too! As one of the homeschool days out of the house, we attended a Community Bible Study where the kids had a bible program and wonderful teachers. I was hearing the Spirit of God lead me to prophesy! I remember one lady was battling with breast cancer, and God told me to remind her of the story of Moses in Exodus 17:11-16. This was the story of the battle against the Amalekites. Moses was getting tired, so Aaron and Hur held up Moses' hands to keep the Israelites winning. The Lord is our Banner, he goes before us and prepares the way to our victory! Sometimes, we need others to hold our arms up so we can win. I'm still in connection with this precious lady who is cancer-free and living strong for the Lord because she certifies me in CPR every two years. During this time, when our kids were very young, this bible study group encouraged me greatly. We also loved going to Free Chapel Church because it was a spirit-filled church! The kids' program was awesome! My best friend and I served in the children's program, and I still have the free CDs of the sermons. Jentezen Franklin taught a lot about trusting the Holy Spirit as your guide. My faith and peace of mind felt sound, and the evidence from God was a daily occurrence. During this time, I was in great shape! Our home was known as Camp because not only did all my nephews come over for days, but we had friends over at least once a week. We had four-wheelers, a trampoline, a pool, a 250 ft. zip line, indoor forts, a workout room, and lots of outdoor field games like softball and kickball. Fourth of July fireworks were like Stone Mountain's fireworks show over our three acres. Those days made me feel so blessed! Family memories and connections with friends helped me live with purpose. My grandmother was living through the youth of our kids, their friends, and our nephews. She was always helpful!

I did not have a career with benefits, but Bobby promised to always take care of me. I helped him with his lawn maintenance business, served his nutritional and affection needs, homeschooled our kids all the way through high school, served students and parents in our homeschool groups, worked as a fitness instructor and did my best to train my mind in the way of the truth and the life of God.

Like Charles Dickens quoted, "It was the best of times, it was the worst of times." Since gas prices were rising, we changed back to attending Bethlehem Church, and the country was becoming racially divided. Due to an unfortunate family death, our CC Director had to find someone to replace her, and our community was dispersing because many of us had kids moving into high school. There was a shift happening. Change can be for the good, but it's determined by how you look at it. Perception is everything to your inner peace, but it took years for me to find that clarity. Busyness is a dangerous place to be! If it wasn't for my Nanny and Christ, I think Bobby and I could have separated. I never rested my brain. From 5 am to 11 pm,

I had to keep it all together. Our homeschool days were amazing for about ten years until I started working a lot, lost focus, and could not manage the many responsibilities of five jobs. I gave away my joy by focusing on limiting beliefs instead of my first ministry to love my spouse. I could have ministered to him with the service of unconditional love as a good wife. I could have loved him 'as he was.' "God demonstrates his own love for us in this: While we were still sinners, Christ died for us."[16] But, I was irritated about my husband's self-care habits and forgetfulness and this resulted in some unhealthy thoughts in my head against him. I had formed a weapon against him. Toxic thoughts.

Only a couple of years later, our church was on the brink of a big revival, just after our pastor decided to leave the pastoral seat for a government seat. Our worship leader at Bethlehem was our pastor and worship leader for a while, and he ushered in the Holy Spirit in a mighty way. It was exciting! This was just before Obama took office. I started a prayer walk, like the Jericho walk in the bible. I remember the week before National Day of Prayer in 2008, we believed for walls of Jericho (enemy assignments) to come down. A powerful anointing poured over me again. Sometimes, I look back to this day as the start of my calling to help people believe in the Holy Spirit as the healer and deliver from troubles. No matter the circumstances, we could either be victims or victors. I had wristbands made with C5 on them. It stood for Commission of Grace. The wristbands were used by the prayer walkers who agreed to do Jericho walks. The word commission must have been a word with an assignment because it came to me like

---

[16] Romans 5:8 NIV

some random thought. Jesus' commission was a restoration of the lost. I kept the belief in Unity through Diversity from my sorority college days. The C5 Prayer Walk's mission was to help unite churches of differing races, neighborhoods, and schools. I remember being with a Christian leader from our local church who left many footprints of impact. She joined us at the flagpole on school property. One clear, beautiful day, we walked around a school, stopped to pray at the pole, and looked up after praying. There in the sky was the most beautiful circle green and pink rainbow. I had never seen a rainbow like that before! I felt like God was speaking to us! A week later, I was flipping open my bible, and the scripture Revelation 4:3 caught my attention: "And the one who sat there had the appearance of Jasper and Ruby. A rainbow that shone like an emerald encircled the throne." That was evidence to me that God heard our prayer. As a group, we prayed for grace, God's unmerited favor, to cover our nation. It was less than a decade following that Holy Spirit-filled day that this godly woman, after knee surgery, unexpectedly went home to her heavenly father. During this Holy Spirit movement, I was at a local Baptist Church, and people were standing to give their testimony of God's work in their lives. The pastor called on everyone except me, although I clearly knew the Lord told me to stand! I felt my heart beating fast and the Spirit of God pulling me to my feet. That pastor looked straight at me and then asked everyone to sit. I felt rejection, but I had to remember that even Jesus was rejected and despised. The movie *Facing the Giants* came out a couple of years before and it inspired me to stand against the odds. There was a scene of a football player doing the death crawl. He was crawling blindfolded with a 160 lb. player on his back, and the coach was yelling, 'Keep going! You're almost there.' When the student exhausted all his physical might, he thought he had only traveled 30 yards, and he had travelled the entire field. If we were blindfolded to our circumstances, I wonder how far we could travel. I know it is the voice we hear in our heads that is either keeping us defeated or keeping us focused on winning. Give yourself grace or believe in the grace from God. Another part of "Facing the Giants", which was significant for me, was when the team yelled, 'Stonewall!' Jesus wanted us to believe that no weapon formed against us will prosper.[17] I can tell you that the enemy of my flesh wanted me to have some stonewalls or heart walls about that pastor at the local Baptist Church so that nothing, not even the Holy Spirit, could get through! After these apostolic movements, there were about 10 years of silence when I didn't feel anointed. This was only a test! I'm so glad I had this test back then because rejection does make you stronger if you choose to get back up and fight for Love.

After the 2008 National Day of Prayer, I lost my determination to continue. I put away the C5 terry cloth wristbands. A shift was happening, not externally, but in my thoughts and emotions. Where the mind goes, the body follows. I needed to grow and learn patience, but I didn't know it would take over 10 years! The words we tell ourselves can build or break us. I remained a faithful believer but felt hopeless that God would use me. But I knew God used Deborah to lead an army! All I knew was to focus on ministry to the two precious gifts from heaven above which God gave us. To teach them to love. I did my best, although there were times when I did not feel valued, confident, or at peace.

---

[17] Isaiah 54:17

Perspective of gender roles may create conflict in a family. Bobby was taught that the outside was the man's job, and the inside was the woman's job. How respect is shown, how people work together, and how one gains confidence matters to the whole family. Each family member may have certain responsibilities but still lack the feeling of connection as a team. The mistake is to find identity and value in the belief you hold too tightly. I see this mistake in my own life when I held onto the belief I gained as a woman martial artist that I could (if I had to) defend myself. I loved feeling tough. This hurt my marriage relationship.

I believe respect is caught, not just taught. Some would say respect is earned, but that's a world concept. Often, we become the environments we are raised in. It's important to learn to follow the opposite way if your environment is disrespectfully toxic. "Bad company corrupts good character."[18] From my perception, our kids witnessed my emotions in response to the atmosphere, discomfort and division of beliefs about the world we were experiencing. They saw the real world, and we could not hide our tensions. Sometimes, I wondered if they thought it would be better if we divorced. That was what my husband questioned about his parents because of their lack of love and respect for one another. Fortunately, our kids did finally witness love and respect between us. It was only at random times that tensions were heightened.

God was allowing me to learn and unlearn throughout my life, almost like trying on clothes and changing them often. It was a daily cycle. I also learned from one karate instructor that

---

[18] 1 Corinthians 15:33

slow is fast, and fast is slow. If you want to train well, you must go slow and practice until it is on autopilot. "Where there is no vision, the people perish."[19] If one can slow down enough to visualize it in the mind, then he can run with perseverance. Ask yourself daily, "I don't hear fear, do I?" If you do, calm yourself down and reinforce a new perception. What world do you see? My Nanny believed there was hope as long as anyone remained alive. Respecting the community means you cannot allow a closed hand. Open hands include the ability to give and receive love.

I remember being at a homeschool convention, and God speaking into my spirit the word 'Open hand,' and this was another confirmation that we were supposed to do this style of karate. When a person is in the flow of life, not indecisive and questioning everything, there is so much more joy and power! "The joy of the Lord is my strength."[20]

Karate taught me so much about life, including respect. I respect the ones who get back up from a loss and never quit trying to get it right. The style of our karate was 'open hand,' and that is important because I knew God destined our family to live this way, never to hold anything of this world too tightly. Many mysterious signs directed us to be open-handed Symbolically, the heart is about the size of a fist and blocked valves (doors) leads to death. A closed fist represents attack and anger. You cannot gain peace with this fighting mindset.

One of my favorite things I learned in Tang Soo Do was the Pyung Ahn Hyung five forms before the black belt ranking

---

[19] Proverbs 29:18 KJV

[20] Nehemiah 8:10

because these are foundational forms, just like Kindergarten through fifth grade. There is symbology in our karate forms from Tang Soo Do that points to my sorority mascot (turtle) and being a woman who works in the house to balance the home.

"The Pyung Ahn Hyung were created by Master Itosu Yasutsune from Okinawa in around 1870. The term "Pyung Ahn" translates as "peaceful confidence". The two characters of the word can be broken down further. Pyung is made up of characters meaning a 'scale' and 'equal weight'. Ahn is made up of 'house' and 'woman'. These hyung characterize the turtle and are designed to teach balance and confidence."[21]

Since these were the first five, and five is my number, I knew God had my attention! When we sparred in karate, we shouted "Hei" when we attacked our opponent. This is the sound of the fifth letter of the Hebrew alphabet, which means Grace. Our instructors were Christian twins who had great character. I wanted our kids to learn from people like them.

From the public view, we had a perfect family and marriage! HAHA! No marriage is perfect! It takes work, but our marriage suffered because our love tanks were empty due to due to emotional distance and disagreements about the distribution of finances. To fill your love tank, you cannot spend more time with others and withhold love from your spouse (closed fist). Our earthly biological fathers cannot fill our love tanks. I remember when a friend asked me to do The Love Dare book by Alex Kendrick. I failed because I could

---

[21] https://lowsmartialarts.com/tang-soo-do-forms/

not even get through the first few days. The devil, or even your own ego, always wants us to be busy and withhold love and retain grudges because this grieves the Holy Spirit. My husband worked a lot between two full-time jobs for almost 20 years. His body was exhausted, and often, I embraced the burden of his silent treatment and passive-aggressive emotions. I multi-tasked non-stop between five part-time jobs therefore, we experienced the effects of marital distance! My husband had to get to work at 5 am. His alarm would begin going off at 4 am, and then he would wake up late, speed to work, and be so stressed all day because retail is not easy work. I only stressed him more when I tried to help him get out the door on time, yet he wanted help. I felt he was bitter about any help from me. I was truly trying to be supportive of him, but it did not matter because I was not working in retail or in the elements of weather to even begin to understand. I loved living in a Christian bubble, but this made Bobby feel like he missed out on a lot of our pleasures. That was the way he saw it. He suffered for our pleasure.

Homeschooling the kids and maintaining contentment in my marriage was hard because I did not take my thoughts captive, meditate day and night on God's truth, nor did I fully believe God has his hand in my marriage. Things between us really heated up when I took a "real job" at a local Christian school two days a week while also teaching our high school kids and a group of Classical Conversations kids one day a week! The money was not much, but the titles gave me a sense of accomplishment. Again, Band-Aids! They are never satisfied! Was I ever going to learn? I was in fight/flight mode. Overthinking anything could cause more fear and paralysis, so it is best to trust your gut feeling and test your motives when you make decisions. If you go against God, your peace is at risk since you may be operating from the flesh (ego), and when you come back to God your surrender feels like a band-aid removal to your ego. The ego wants to keep the band-aid because it boasts in all its accomplishments. Humility hurts the ego.

We truly are creatively complex creatures of habit. Our habits may or may not define who we are. If our habits control us, it could be an addiction. People who have addictions are very defensive and judgmental when confronted. When I would sense something was off, I'd ask Bobby, "How are you?" and he'd reply, "Fine. It's all good." This response did not fit his demeanor. He was not fine. Bobby worked all the time, and it consumed his identity. I did the same thing. It was more comfortable to work than to spend time with each other. We chose to work. It gave him his identity as a provider. It gave me my identity as significant. In his perspective, a father who did not provide was not a father. The problem may be the definition we give things. What does a provider do? Is it only related to money? What is a good enough marriage? Is it only two people agreeing to work and live together? That's a negative! If two people have different definitions and are working toward the same goal, then the goal will be hard to achieve because they both believe differently and are operating by work only. A shared vision is key to a shared mission. These types of issues with corrupted foundations and definitions have created a whole host of divisions in our world. I was on the edge of extreme stress and mental breakdown because I wanted happiness. By the end of my son's seventh-grade year and my daughter's tenth-grade year, I was struggling to see how I was going to finish the race (to successful education) well. I knew I was meant to persevere and build my character, but I wanted to give up! I felt fear, but I was fighting hard to keep my faith and persevere through the tensions of change and pressures at home. I had an escape plan, but Bobby had a "suck it up" plan, understanding that this was just part of life. I could hear him saying, "Get over it!" I knew how blessed we were to have healthy kids, but Bobby was not aware at the time that our daughter was struggling with an eating disorder. I wanted to reset my life because I felt I was not going to obtain a sound mind without a reset of my circumstances. I feared I'd never measure up to meet my husband's needs or the respect as a mom compared to other moms who worked. I was lacking the spiritual keys of faith, hope, and love (in and toward myself)! I was desperate for change under all the pressure to perform.

To add to the emotional crisis, one Sunday morning, my grandmother had a car wreck on her way to church. We were already into the worship at our church service with our phones on silent. She tried to call us but to no avail. The officer was so kind; he brought her home since it was only 1 mile from our house. That event was the beginning of a decline in her health. She told me that when the officer asked her to slide over to the passenger seat so she could exit her Cadillac, she panicked because she thought he would see, as she stated, 'everything she has.' (That was her undergarments because she was wearing a long dress). Obviously, she was not badly hurt, although she was miraculously spared since a standard truck T-boned her vehicle at 45 miles/hour at the top of a dangerous hill. It was about one year later that she passed away, but her last year on earth was undoubtedly her favorite experience of her elder years. She enjoyed serving the seniors at the local

Senior Center. She delayed going there for about a year because she believed she wasn't old, although she was 84! I remember her feeling like she did not have a calling or ministry, but her last year on earth fulfilled her calling and purpose to serve others. My grandmother had many doctor's appointments, which I never minded taking her to, but one appointment was very strange. This was an appointment for her leg, that had a small wound that would not heal after one year from her car accident. The wound care center had been packing it with the silver cream. We returned home from the wound care center that evening, and before we exited the car, she started to cry. She said, "Honey, I never want to burden you." I replied, "You never do! I love you and want to take care of you." Later that evening, while doing math homework with my son, my grandmother went into cardiac arrest! I performed CPR, the EMTs arrived, we went to the hospital, and an hour later, I was told she did not survive! It was tragic! It was confusing. I had to call my mom and tell her the news, and it was like time just stopped for me. I had not cried until that moment. I had no one at the hospital to comfort me until Mom arrived. She was an hour away, but within minutes, she and my stepdad were there. I had to regroup myself because it was such an adrenaline rush. Everything was strange to me, and it was hard to understand God's plan. I had to let go of the fear that her death was affected by my performance. She lived with us for seven years, died on the day of the Jewish day of Atonement, and entered another world without much pain and suffering. It was too quick! During the last year of her life, she enjoyed the Senior Center activities, went to Pennsylvania, and local rodeo! Though I wish she could've lived with us longer, I believe our days are numbered and ordered. Numbers not only have meaning, but they may also bring comfort. The number 7 means complete or perfect. Her passing felt like a piece of perfection left my life. It took about one year, just like when my cousin passed, to retrain my peace. I made the decision to quit CC and teach Latin at an accredited homeschool program and enroll our son for his final high school years, hoping to release some pressure. Dogs are typically good company for a family. Just before my Nanny passed away, we took in a stray little dog. Nanny named him Curly Top. He was a great comfort to our son! The hardest loss was our first family dog. My husband had to lay him to rest in our backyard. After Jonah's passing, my husband wanted a guard dog. So, I went to the pound by myself. The dog I picked was going to be euthanized and Bobby wanted a guard dog. This dog was sweet, and she was the Pitbull that my husband requested, but she was also very skittish because she was abused. I later found out she had heartworms. Bobby was disappointed that I made the decision to bring Chex into our home because I did it without him. I emotionally struggled with thoughts of defeat when anyone constructively criticized any of my heartfelt decisions. When I felt rejection or got my feelings hurt, I would automatically be triggered to respond by comforting my flesh either through food or with people who would listen to my stress. I also struggled when Bobby withdrew communication, so my reactions and Bobby's reactions were just catalysts for more hurt. C.S. Lewis quoted, "Spiteful words can hurt your feelings, but silence breaks your heart." When Chex became ill, it was all up to me to carry her 65lb body to the vet for euthanasia. My husband wanted a guard dog, and he thought Chandler would feel comfortable if he had another dog. Off they went to the dog shelter! They returned with two puppies that didn't grow out of their puppy stage for two years. They practically tore up our house like goats that eat an entire yard of grass. They even ate the arm off my new outdoor swinging rocker. The stress of their destruction almost sent me over the edge! Bobby and I had differing perspectives, and separation was still a topic. It was hard for me to find contentment as a homeschool mom, which should have been easy knowing I felt called to this, but in my head, I struggled because my husband would get so frustrated with his unsatisfying life and all the government secrecy stuff going on with President Trump. We knew something needed to change because the silent resistance was unbearable with two new dogs and the summer harvest demands from our home garden.

Sometimes, all we see is the problem. The one who sees the problem is like the one who only sees the Veil. Spiritually, I'm talking about the old church, the church of law. When Jesus died, the veil was torn. This made it possible for us to see because things were coming to light. Just like scales falling off our eyes as stated in the book of Acts 8:17-18. It's that point of knowing what you should be focusing on. I shared what I call the Medicine Ball Problem with my clients. As a trainer, my clients are always assuming that I have one more rep or one more exercise for them before they are finished. Assumptions are based on things we either have experienced or see as a problem. If I set up a workout with the medicine ball (MB) on the floor and never used it, my client would assume the reason for the MB, right? My assumptions and illusions led me down the path of fear too many times. The stress during the present workout would escalate because of the fear of the next exercise that may be a challenging task. The point here is sometimes we get distracted by things that are not relative to the present and it causes us to function without peaceful emotions.

About five years before the COVID-19 pandemic, I had an old friend reach out to me about working as a fitness instructor again. I took the job and helped her start a gym closer to home. I loved this old connection and began thriving again. During the three years of working in that fitness atmosphere, I was gaining a worldly identity and loved the attention as a well-known trainer on Facebook in my area. I started to get back into great shape, too! I was happy about being gone at 4 am every morning because that way, I would not start my day judging my husband. I wish I could undo all the times I judged others from a place of fear or defense for my comfort. I loved that job and the clients I trained, but God had a new vision for me. I believe he wanted me free.

I enjoyed serving people who wanted help, and this became a way of satisfaction for me. I had stopped training in karate because my plate was full of working and finishing the call of homeschooling. I wanted to complete my bachelor's degree, thinking I could do accounting and help my husband with his business. I went to a local college for a time. Again, I was trying to perform, hoping to be loved more. My boss claimed that accounting did not align with my heart's desire, which I agreed. What I did not know was that God had a plan for me a few years later, but this vision really started years before I worked there. My 5 am session was a special group to me. I gave away some old wristbands that I had from the past when I did the Jericho prayer walk, and we took a picture for our Facebook page. I knew God had given me a vision for a C5 ministry, but my heart was broken after a few years of working for my friend at her gym. Interestingly, I lost my voice just before leaving that job. Did you know that your voice is also connected with your vocation? I didn't see the spiritual shift until later when God showed me the growth that would come from the change.

Our daughter finished high school on her own by completing CLEP exams for college and high school credit. She achieved all the necessary credits to graduate in 2017, plus some college credits to transfer to Georgia Gwinnett College. We enrolled her with other homeschoolers to walk and graduate with honors. Georgia Homeschool Education Association accepted mom's diploma! I knew this girl had a calling in her life, but I was not sure about her decision to attend dental hygiene school. Bobby's sister was a hygienist. She applied to two hygiene colleges and was denied, albeit she was the 15th in line of the 14 open positions for acceptance out of 300. She thought she'd be called if someone dropped out. Meanwhile, she randomly changed her mind and applied to nursing school. With the first application, she was accepted! I guess that was divine! Looking back, I was an unqualified nurse after my mom's wreck, so for her to desire nursing was kind of a cool coincidence since she would be an officially qualified nurse! Our daughter has a divine connection that sometimes intimidates me. I've always felt like she is my teacher, even though, as her homeschool mom, I was the teacher. I learned more about myself and God when I homeschooled, and she schooled me! That was the birth pains before the miracle! This beautiful child has grown in wisdom and will succeed in her life. She is a master of her thought life! I can't wait to see what comes of her since the doctors had thought something was wrong with her brain when I was pregnant. God is a miracle worker! Thank God we did not keep any attachments to fear. She is manifesting abundance by the power of the mind!

We enrolled our son in a home school program where I taught Latin, and then we enrolled him at a local college after tenth grade to finish high school through Dual Enrollment. When our son graduated high school, we had to deal with the COVID-19 world pandemic. During this time, my daughter took a break from nursing school. Once God confirmed her desire, she applied for reacceptance into the nursing program, with confidence from the Lord that this was her route for her bachelor's degree. She was accepted without any issues. My emotions were all over the place as I was looking for external approval and admiration for my investment as a homeschool mom. This is not right. We should not look for approval outside ourselves. It may feel good to our ego, but it truly never satisfies the peaceful assurance we can have from the Lord. Even though we were in a pandemic, we held our son's graduation ceremony at our house, and we broke all the rules with about 45 people!

I am so proud of our son's hard work, as well as the many projects he did at home, including raising forty chickens and the remodel of our kitchen cabinets and living room furniture with his dad's help. His dad taught him those uncommon Gen Z work ethics and how to be mechanical. This boy taught himself how to install a lift on his truck, too. He is so talented! Before he left home, he worked for 2 Brother Septic which is a Christian company in GA. Troy and Dawson gave Chandler some spiritual teachings that I believe made him into a kind and confident man. I wanted him to complete a bachelor's degree, but he chose a career as an electrical lineman. When our son was nineteen years old, I learned that his name meant candle-maker. I guess God had predestined his name when we named him! As a hands-on learner, he always learned best by doing projects, not reading books. He went to Southeast Lineman Training Center in Trenton, GA and graduated in the Spring. He started a job as an apprentice lineman, living on his own at age 19, paying for two vehicles and his own cell phone, cooking and cleaning, and the list of his manly competence grew. I could not be prouder! I love telling the story of how one of my clients had an apartment in Calhoun, GA, where his first contract job was located. My client told me he felt like he just needed to hold on to the apartment for a little while longer, but he didn't know that God had a plan for my son there! It's so cool how God speaks to his people!

Dream big and never attach to fearful outcomes because whatever happens will be better than your greatest fear! If you set goals with timelines, force them to happen, and then miss the goal, then you may possibly fall into a deep depression because of the attachment to the expectation. God's ways are open-handed, never on a deadline. I believe that is why he told me years ago 'open hand.' Don't hold onto hope you have for some outcome, let go and let God determine the outcome in due time. Our timing is not God's timing, so we would only frustrate our peace if we quit because of our impatience to God's timing. When we go with the flow, allowing God's Spirit to carry us through life, as we trust the Holy Spirit, we learn a lot more about our purpose! It's like resting on the clouds! Wish that was possible! Or maybe it's like floating on a raft, but when we are not in the flow with life, we are living with resistance due to striving so hard. To understand and interpret every trauma or challenge requires micromanaging and this is like the saying 'analysis causes paralysis.' It's important to see the big picture too. I'm a vision and analogy type of a person. I want to understand things. The thoughts I meditated upon caused deeper roots of fear or just deeper roots in my own understanding.

How to Solve Problems

It's important to give careful attention to our thoughts but not to boosting your egoic thoughts. The ability to process thought when we are still is a great practice. If you want to heal, you must retrain your thought life, shift it, recode it, and add value to the new perception. Basing one's self-worth on past outcomes or measurable future goals may do more harm. A person who controls and manipulates their circumstances or people may be afraid of losing since it is a controlling spirit they're operating from. Control is a power given to God; we are truly never able to control anything except possibly our thoughts. When we hear our own thoughts, it's our own voice speaking to us, playing out different conversations in our minds. This is a natural phenomenon. This process is called an internal monologue. It is, however, not common that the Spirit of God speaks to us. Some people experience it, and some don't, and that must not be something we fear. Your mind can be noisy, with positive and negative thoughts. But if you're struggling with negative, repetitive thoughts that are holding you back from living the life you want, it's time to act. Recognizing your "Inner Critic" is a major step in the right direction, and it's not something that many people are aware of. It's like intuitive eating, not many people are responding to their hunger and satisfaction cues. However, simply recognizing your Inner Critic is not enough. You need to learn how to change the way you think and respond to that voice automatically. This can be difficult, but it's possible with some effort and determination. You can rewire your automatic response and retrain your brain. Neuroplasticity is like creating new thought channels in your brain. Positive affirmations and self-talk or creativity are healthy for your mind. We are unique image bearers of Christ. Image, imagination, and imagery these all create pictures in our minds. The illusions we create within us could be positive and refreshing or a natural bent toward the common culture. Training your mind to believe in healthy images can be a challenge. Occasionally, our mental chatter becomes negative. We often punish ourselves for the smallest failures, talk ourselves out of taking chances or become trapped in a cycle of anxiety or guilt. God wants us to live free of condemnation, so it's important to capture and release toxic energy. All these things can prevent us from reaching our full potential. We are not products of our environment. Our environment could have the potential to shift us into any direction, and it's your choice to capture the image you want for yourself. There is one method I have found helpful. The "Notice-Shift-Rewire" strategy is a powerful mindfulness tool that can help you stay present in each moment, increase your attention and productivity, and improve your overall satisfaction with life. How it works is that first, you take a moment to notice when you're getting caught up in thoughts about the past or future. You just stop your mind wandering. Then, shift your focus back to the present moment, maybe by standing outside on solid ground in nature and breathing in thankfulness. I once read that seventeen seconds is the cap time to shift toxic thoughts before they control you in a downward spiral. Finally, rewire your brain by focusing on something positive and building a new healthy image about the subject. The Notice-Shift-Rewire strategy is undoubtedly a great mindfulness activity that can only benefit you if you practice it. You can do this anywhere and whenever you want. Whether you're at the gas pump, shopping for groceries, at home, or in your bed, you can rewire. As Joe Dispenza says, "Nerves that fire together, wire together." Unlike forms of yoga meditation, you don't need to take extra time out of your day to implement this. It's a practice you can do 10, 20, or even 50 times a day without stopping everything else in your everyday life commitments. Our minds are designed for new knowledge, however, a double-minded person, one who exhausts herself/himself between love and fear, may struggle to rewire until their practice becomes more routine in the Spirit instead of just the flesh. I've dealt with this fire-rewire issue almost all my life! The thought life needs to be analyzed so you can fire bad thoughts and rewire new ones! Scripture tells us to set our minds on things above, and to daily renew our minds.[22]

Life may feel like a cycle of faith and unbelief, with the hope of becoming stable in mind. I had unbelief and fear thoughts in my mind repeatedly. For example, I kept speaking about my issues (as my truth), but I preached God's love and forgiveness. You see how frustrating this was in my body to say one thing and speak to myself differently. I know, it is so common! I believe our mental health suffers because our truth, or whatever we keep speaking, does not align with the belief we want for truth. Oneness is when like attracts like, but I had opposite voices of double-mindedness! I thought that if I made money, my husband would love and appreciate me more. That was just a lie I believed as the truth. This is the hamster wheel of lies. I didn't want to idol money; I just wanted a little more

---

[22] Col 3:2, Rom 12:2

to support my whole family. I wanted more peace within. After my experience working for my friend's fitness business, I decided I would give my dream of having my own gym a chance. During the first year of owning C5 Fitness, I studied an entire year and completed eight National Certifications in record time! Bobby told me he was proud of me, but I had a problem believing his words because my income had not soared. So here again, another band-aid! I started working as a server at a local fine dining restaurant and made incredibly fast money. Just before I took the server job, my husband quit his primary job of 20 years. It was good for him, good for me, but not good emotionally for either of us. At the restaurant, I tried to witness my faith, but slowly, I was becoming weaker in my walk with the Lord. I was drinking a little alcohol almost five days a week, I was in physical pain, and very physically tired. I'd work at my gym from 4 am to 9 am, sometimes work at the local hospital in the inpatient rehab, come home to take a short nap, and then go to the restaurant until about 10 pm. My hands started to fall asleep, I had neck pain, and I also had a bad heel spur that made it nearly impossible to keep working other jobs, including the job I took as a server.

Bobby had to regroup his thoughts about himself, and I experienced a year in his shoes by working 60 + hours in the world. Unfortunately, I struggled to feel content and happy with myself, although I should have been proud of myself for all I did and who I was pleasing! I had pleased my husband! But that still didn't make me happy. Remember, money does not solve problems when your relationship with God and your family is not at peace!

How to Solve Problems

Knock, knock. Who's there? Problems. Problems who? Math problems. Go away, I got my own problems. LOL. When your life is not adding up, it's time to pause, process, and petition. Take your thoughts on trial. Perspective is either your peace or your power.

Understanding your capacity to reform your emotions begins with recognizing that our emotions are just responses to the signals or thoughts we perceive to be true at the time. Perception shifts when we have a new image. We must be careful about the signals we are sending through our bodies. This means that you must take responsibility for your thoughts, actions, and emotions. Reforming our inner dialogue to recognize our current perspective, then refocusing on what is true without emotional attachments, could return your internal peace. When you have this deep faith-filled belief in truth, not just images, you'll be able to stay positive and recover quickly after any failure. Everything else in your life will fall into place from there.

In the book by Dr. Caroline Leaf called *Switch on Your Brain,* she mentions a metacognitive mind-mapping approach (MMA). This method may help you select your thoughts more carefully. She also has an app called Neuro Cycle that has a five-step process to help you take control of your thoughts. Remember, what you focus on will grow in power. It's like a consuming fire that brands your DNA.

Untrained thoughts followed by action are like children without instruction, foolish. Where the mind goes, the body follows. Or, as my karate instructor stated, *'Where the head goes, the body follows.'* In my thirties, I took up karate lessons with my kids for 10 ½ years. We were taught to keep your minds and emotions separated when sparring. If your pride or ego captures thoughts and forms you into becoming a bully, you would have to sit out of sparring until you regain control over yourself. Time out is super important. It helps you get a better vision. Proverbs 29:18 states how important it is to have a vision, or you may perish. When we are centered in Christ with our thoughts, we are not rude and disrespectful. Thoughts left to themselves, untamed, turn into destructive emotions. Emotions that are not dealt with will deal with you (in return) at some point in your life.

Emotions Matter

We first have a feeling that then turns into thoughts, and thoughts convert into emotions. Emotions that are not metabolized, kind of like food that comes in but doesn't exist, will eventually cause toxicity and are warning signs we need to heed. As a personal trainer, I tell my clients you have two choices when it comes to food: waste it or waist it (belly fat). It's okay to throw it away if there is no benefit to you, but take only what you know is a good measure for your needs. Hoarding is unhealthy because it symbolizes the trapped emotion of scarcity. Sometimes, we hoard our feelings and our stories, and this only creates more pain, whether physical or emotional. Everyone's pain story is valuable, but if you are not healing from retelling the story, then "let that shit go!" Garbage is garbage. *The Body Keeps the Score* by Dr. Bessel van der Kolk is a helpful resource for understanding what I call the garbage in, garbage out concept. If a traumatic thought gets trapped as a memory in the DNA, and science shows this is possible, then it can affect generations.

Jesus spoke about thoughts being just as bad as the action itself. (See Matt 5:28 NIV.) I believe some thoughts are fickle, but when those thoughts become emotions, then they have the potential for damaging consequences. People need the freedom to discuss their thoughts and emotions, but we don't do this because of our pride and unbelief.

You cannot shift the direction of your thoughts with the same current of your thoughts. More knowledge may provide some power, but just like a vacuum, the power is only possible when the source makes a connection for use. Knowledge is like power but there are times when we need to unplug; we need to choose to learn or unlearn too. We must correctly practice good instruction if we want it caught in the limbic system and hippocampus, the retaining centers of the brain. I had to unlearn some common reactions and fears.

Consistently spending time to seek your thoughts and mind patterns and to know yourself through journaling and maybe reading texts that challenge your thoughts are a couple of examples for self-love and healing. Some strategies for healing areas of your life, such as self-condemnation, may include positive visualizations, journaling, meditating on truths from God's word, affirming yourself, and staying plugged into inspirational stories. Through these actions, you may experience revelation about what gifts God has given you to process the hard emotional times. As you do these actions, you may also discover the truth! The heart works like separating the parts of an onion. The strongest and most potent part of an onion is the core. When you get tired of being what everyone else thinks you should be, you finally make the decision to be who you were created to be. An onion gives flavor, but it can also make you cry. Finding self-love is emotional. The training is hard. It's like taking an ax to the trunk of a 100-year-old tree and hitting it one last time before you shout, "Timber!" When we uproot old fruit, we have more opportunities for clear perception. Just make sure you are chopping down the right tree! Scripture states we should not conform to the patterns of this world (Rom 12:2). Naturally, we model ourselves after our parents, guardians and superiors. As adults, we may choose to keep or change the pattern, but we must be ready for a challenge because new patterns are often rejected by the culture. It's crazy how our culture has rejected some of the Ancient and most valuable foundations. We can intend to do well, but it's the pattern of our ways that determines the destiny. Change as an adult is a challenge because the patterns are often rooted in the common culture due to fear of being different or odd, so a change may never truly happen. If we do the little challenges that add value, the best is yet to come! Then it's like slicing through soft butter!

Thoughts can be both positive and negative. Every thought has weight, so losing what weighs us down will help us gain peace. Unnecessary thoughts that start to rob you of peace may be a waste of time and energy. That's your abundance! Peace University is a school of thought for how to create abundant living. Have you ever had a list of millions of things to do but can't figure out where to start? You can have that pressure which can lead to stress, but is that always bad? No, however, it is proven that busy people learn to prioritize value. If your value of yourself is external or based on productivity, then stress may be controlling you. If your value is like standing in front of the mirror and asking yourself if you're good enough, then your reflection or image could hurt your self-confidence and self-esteem. I can remember looking into the mirror and saying, "It is safe to love you." This was hard, but it worked for me.

Remember: The only thing in life you can control is yourself, right? Well, this is not 100% accurate. It takes practice to train or control your flesh. If you are training a pet, such as a dog, you must be patient and use commands that are loving and provide dopamine or a reward for continued practice. The same thing goes with your thoughts. When you train your thoughts to align with the positive, the reward follows. I know you can't control what life throws your way, but 99% of the time, you can control how you react to a situation. Once you empower yourself to change the things you can control - your attitude and outlook, for example, only then will you be ready to face whatever challenges come your way with a positive mindset. I had to go deeper than myself due to practicing negatively for far too long. I surrendered, and I had to ask the Spirit for help. I knew I had failed, and I wanted freedom. I could not save myself without the Lord's help.

There will be times in your life that you struggle to love, believe, and do right, but I know the One who wipes away every tear! There is no perfect law or method, although man has created tools to help us. Ultimately, our guide to life is within us, by the born-again spirit of the one true and living God. Whoever rules the mind rules the body. Our minds also control our digestive system. When we allow fear, it often shows up in our intestines. This can cause ulcers in the stomach, too. Make every effort to stop double-mindedness. Living double-minded is not God's will. A dual is a battle between two sources. If you are a divided house within yourself, then there will be a war within your mind. This knowledge could be a powerful method to stop the cycle of negative beliefs. When we surrender one of the powers, such as the one thought that leads to death, then the battle is won. Trust the source of all living things. Even living things have a cycle of life, embracing its seasons. Sometimes bad things happen, but it's how we reframe or correct our beliefs that matters. God knows everything, and His plans are better than ours once we let go of our selfishness and egoic satisfaction.

Retrain your Mind

Replacing negative thoughts is not really replacing or trading with more positive thoughts. It's more like overriding them, overflowing them with more abundance and life-giving thoughts. When negative ideas invade your mind, let the Holy Spirit perform what you are unable to do completely on your own. Ask the Spirit to be your guide. Be open to the supernatural. Only when we let go of our poisonous thinking will we be able to receive God's blessings with open hands and hearts. Fight the 6-inch war of your thoughts as many times as necessary. This is a conscious decision to obey God and honor others as well as you do yourself. True living happens when you put truth training in your mind.

From my own practice, just claiming positive affirmations over my mind and body was not enough. What worked for me was to keep building a foundation in the Scriptures, like concrete. What you repeat, you get to keep. Hiding the living Word in my heart, even when I didn't feel like it was making a difference, eventually transformed my heart into a life I wanted to share. What you focus on becomes your truth. The sword of the Spirit, which is the Word of God, is one of the weapons for spiritual battle. It is alive, active, and strong in the battleground of our thoughts. To disrupt the cycle of negative thinking in your life, start meditating on the scriptures first thing in the morning and before going to bed. We used the Charlotte Mason method for memorizing scripture and great proverbs. The card box was set up with 4 tabs: Daily, weekly, monthly, and yearly. It helped us put into practice life-giving words. We chose only one verse and worked on it until it was memorized. Then, we moved that verse to once a week. If we could not recall the verse, then we moved it back to the daily. As we trained our brains and disciplined our bodies, we did not have to frequent the daily recall as often. As you use scripture to train your thinking, remember to fully rely on the Holy Spirit to guide you. Maybe there is a scripture that really speaks to you in a certain season but not so much in other seasons. When you meditate day and night on winning the war between your ears, then you will begin to lay this strong foundation for overcoming negative thoughts. They will eventually stay at bay, where you can just recognize them from far away!

Understand your Ability to Select What you want to Focus on

We are often presented with difficult decisions to make, with several options or pathways before us. It can be overwhelming, and we may feel bewildered and hope to get some advice from others. To make those decisions, we rely on our own experience, the knowledge of others, and our reasoning talents. Our reactions to those important choices shape our lives and frame meaning into who we are. Decisions to follow or not to follow. God is always calling us to follow him, but making the decision is a challenge because it means we must leave behind the things that hinder our growth that were pleasures of the flesh. Choosing the direction that leads to an abundant life means you must take negative thoughts on trial. Ask the thought, 'Where did you come from?'

Capturing our own ideas entails recognizing and noticing them, as well as refusing to allow poisonous thoughts to run wild, build barriers, define identities, or drive decisions. Capturing ideas is submitting them to Christ rather than allowing them to fester or engrave them in our brains. I have a 17-second practice for this. If I don't capture and rewire the thought from negative to positive, speaking out loud, then it will fester or spiral the wrong way and affect my day.

Pray Out Loud

In this strategy, you will be making a confession of the truth. The confessions will bring healing to your soul. Your boldness in the spoken Word of God will feel so empowering! Declare victory over the issue. Have you ever seen the movie "War Room" with Priscilla Shirer? This lady has authority! I love her! The Lord cannot deny His Word because he is the Word. See John 1:1-2. When we pray the scriptures out loud, we are activating our faith and making agreements that cannot return void. Prayer is a great tool for combating our human inclination to concentrate on the reality of our senses. Many negative thinking patterns go beneath our radar and are typically habitual tendencies that are difficult to break. Jesus claims in Matthew 11:29 that his burden is light. So, in other words, he can handle your hardships. Boldly, ask Christ to give you the ability to identify misdirected thoughts and make better decisions, ones that honor Him, others, and yourself. Prayer breaks strongholds! Psalm 91 is a great passage for protection and guidance. A stronghold is often an emotionally deep-rooted issue that can only be broken by intentional prayer, faith, and works of love. Love is a verb, so you must do hard things (pray) to break the chain of the negative. Use your words and pray a new confession out loud.

Stop the Negativity

You will waste your life source if you remain negative. Think of it like choosing death. Is that what you want? Negative self-talk is destructive. We draw more negativity into our lives when we dwell on the negative. Don't be your own enemy, giving power to destructive thoughts. Scripture states in Matthew 12:25, "A house divided against itself cannot stand." Paraphrased, if you want the negative to stop, you can't use negative to drive it out. Complaining never solves problems. Jentezen Franklin stated in one of his great sermons, "Be quiet, there is victory in progress!" My Nanny told me several times my life would be better if I would keep my mouth shut. There is power in words, but learning how to use them precisely is the key! My friend told me in 2023 that I talk too much! What she meant was you cannot hear God speak if you are doing all the talking, or even when you think too much with your human understanding. Ephesians 5:15-17 reminds us to be careful and to understand what the Lord's will is. Set a clear boundary with your negative thoughts because living with internal negativity is not the correct direction for freedom. You must change your emphasis to the positive, to the Spirit that gives life, if you want to retrain your brain to retain new thoughts.

We may flourish in the assurance that we are loved, appreciated, and full in Christ when we are free of our negative thought processes. Not having the guidance of the Lord in his Word can often make you dwell in this incessant chattering in your brain. When the Holy Spirit leads us, we have peace because it is not "I" who is doing the action, but the Spirit "I Am" (who I believe in) that is doing it. His creation operates involuntarily when your will has become His will. Be patient in this process because God knows the best timing!

When you are appreciative of yourself and others, fear generally leaves, and love arises. In a heart full of appreciation, there is no place for negative feelings or self-talk. Your beliefs shape your environment, and your beliefs shape your thinking. Unfavorable self-talk can thus lead to negative ideas about yourself and the world, preventing you from attaining your goals. Picture the season of fall in the United States. When leaves fall, picture this as negative thoughts falling off you. Now that is quite beautiful!

When we choose to view the positive, we establish a positive mood loop. What goes around, comes around. It's a manifestation of the law of attraction, and you can utilize it to learn how to quit negative self-talk. In our hurts, we want others to understand our pain story because we believe if they empathize with us, then we will be better, but the problem is that this is attracting a co-dependency to keep talking about our pain story to feel better. This is a distorted love because it is only temporary. No one wants to hear your pain story your entire life!

At times I felt like my life was just a façade, or like a curtain over the real deal. I felt afraid, like I had to pretend, maybe like performers do in a Broadway show. This is common, desiring to be accepted by others as if we lacked something that was necessary for quality living. Truly, we don't lack beneficial things, we just perceive we lack, and therefore, we become sad, withdrawn, or even vengeful. We don't live in a perfect world with perfect people, and there will be suffering. If we never have to suffer, we don't develop character. Maybe this is why we are to love our enemies. My husband, though I thought of him as a villain actually made me stronger becoming more like a hero. Proverbs 27:17 states, *"Iron sharpens iron"*. It's what we do with the suffering that matters. We are not to attack back with vengeance when we are attacked because this would only invite more vengeance. When we follow Jesus as our role model, the guilt and shame of our choices will not haunt us because there will be no shadow since he is the Light. Jesus did the right thing, even when it cost Him His life. I think that one of the most important reasons Jesus sends his Spirit to us is to assist us in making decisions. Just think if he chose to quit because it was too hard to save us. Instead, he ripped the veil because he was that powerful!

So, for the sake of God's sacrifice, it is best to recognize that no one wants you to stay in the pain. Unveil yourself! Empty yourself to your creator and become who he is. He is love. As a child, it's easier to love and forgive. When I was young and innocent, I would talk to everyone, even strangers! I'm naturally a very open person, but fear closed me up to becoming someone I did not recognize anymore. When my own identity as a wife and mother was at a high stress point, I made decisions based on fear. Any decision based on worldly fear will fail. When we operate from fear, we suffer. How long do you want to suffer? I don't believe this is a choice. I mean who wants to suffer, right? The term suffering may imply negative emotions. It's important to consider the effects of fearful emotions before making any decisions. You get to choose your thoughts. So, you ask yourself, has "it" ever happened to you at any stage of your life? What does that fear do to you physiologically or socially? Do you desire to meditate upon this emotion? I allowed a lot of fear to become trapped in my body. But I do believe, by God's grace I'm still leaning into faith. Jesus came to fulfill the law, which was more fear-based, and he came to show us love, forgiveness, and grace. Without fear of death, Jesus overcame the grave. He said his grace is sufficient for us, and we are made perfect in weakness (2 Corinthians 12:9). Suffering not only allows us to grow closer to Christ by learning from His wisdom, but it also permits the life of Christ to be more visible in our own lives. Our difficulties are opportunities to develop our character and move us towards obedience to Christ. Our strength through the challenges provides hope and encouragement to others who may be struggling as well. Suffering may not be pleasant, but it is a part of life that helps us grow and learn. Faith is simple, but we make it harder because we lack wisdom.

    If you know your calling and you are afraid of financial security, then you cannot move to the next level because you have not made sound agreements in alignment with your calling. You may have super sticky adhesives like a Band-aid, and you may not feel comfortable removing them. Sometimes, only the Holy Spirit can remove the divided agreements we've ignorantly fashioned. It may mean pain when God is removing the Band-aid for you. If you don't let false idols go, God will Let it go for you! He will reveal the sin. But don't make the band-aid mistake of replacing the band-aid with another one.

Healing is in the revealing. But it is all for your good! Holding on to the flesh's comfort or any past image is bondage. Be free so that you can live without remembering a painful past. Just because other's stories have formed a fearful image in your mind does not mean that the same outcome will happen for you. The past can be shared if it is a testimony of good news or, used to advance the Kingdom of God within you, or used as a platform to advance your current level. Otherwise, shake it off, pull it off, tear it off. The things that do not help you hinder you. When I allowed myself to be used by God, I was able to break away from the chains that kept me captive. It was a process of training, failing, training, succeeding, and repeating until I had less failures. Honestly, they really were not failures. They were just things and events I learned from.

Now, I have learned that I have the power to activate faith and that is enough power to send fear back to the pit of hell. Someone once told me that if God is not big enough to handle this problem, then he is not God. His teachings tell us to take every thought captive and to surrender it to him because his burdens are light.[23] Years later, after much innocence and ignorance, my perspective about my marriage changed, and I started to heal.

---

[23] 1 Peter 5:7, Matt 11:28-30

Chapter Four
Redemption

I became a Christian after the 1995 accident, but my growth and maturity is an everyday faith journey. The way someone recovers from an identity setback may reflect their belief in a supernatural, limitless God. We can learn how to accept ourselves, even though we were separated by our sin patterns, and we can live with peace in such a diverse world. Transformation happens internally first, and then the story begins. The miracle of the car accidents, angels, healings, and my 1st childbirth were pivotal transitions into true spiritual living. Were we missing these clues to a supernatural world?

Quitting or living in fear only keeps you stuck. No one I have ever met enjoys being stuck. Ivan Tait preached a sermon I will never forget. The title was "I've Never Seen a Vulture Eating a Moving Cow." The title alone reminded me to keep moving because depression and fear could figuratively allow vultures to destroy me. What was meant for bad, such as jealousy, criticism, condemnation, bitterness, and betrayal, may have been part of the villain story, but the hero story must be the ending! Prayer is a way to get your victim's mind from 'stuck' to an 'unstuck' victor! If we don't transform our thoughts, if we quit, or if we walk in fear, then we will miss the way to miracles. When I turned 46 and my husband turned 47, it was the year of our Jubilee! Keep reading, you don't want to miss the miracle!

The direction you go is the choice to follow the voice of love. God is Love. When a person truly knows God's love you can regain natural security. True love is knowing who you are, not who you are expected to become by someone else's standards. Performance fear is no longer allowed to control you! Sometimes, we prioritize these created fears, but this is dangerous. Remember, Love is greater than fear. My journey to self-actualization and understanding started when I became a nobody to the world, died to my ego/flesh, and I finally learned to "be still" at age forty-six. I discovered in the stillness awareness that each stage of my identity crisis was purposed and planned for my benefit. Not everything in this journey of mine is a miracle, but a lot of it is! I gained confidence, lost it, and finally learned to embrace my authentic self! Authenticity is critical to your freedom! Position is just as important. Where you stand will determine the action you take. It's like a see-saw. You can tilt the load when you are in the right position. It takes faith, which is spelled R-I-S-K! Faith is not living realistically, based on human logic. It is living unrealistically and uncommonly. It is trusting in the power of the Holy Spirit, whom you cannot see or control. It may have taken 46 years to become whole because I thought I was too broken, like damaged goods, but after failing at this identity thing for the 100th time, I figured it was time to surrender and accept the fact that God was going to use me to tell His story.

Going back to my first mission, homeschooling. I remember I had taught our kids the Shema found in Deuteronomy 6, which is like the Lord's prayer and mentions loving God with all your heart, soul, mind, and strength. I pressed on in faith, even after many emotional roller coasters, that one day I would give a testimony of my endurance to love and forgive, just as Christ did. We rolled a scroll and put it in a Mezuzah box on our door frame. I didn't know then that the Lord was planting a seed in my heart to remember the foundation to inner peace. "Hear, O Israel: The LORD our God, the LORD is one. Love the LORD your God with all your heart and with all your soul and with all your strength." Love covers a multitude of sins. God is Love. He is enough, even when we feel like we are not. It all started to come together, the puzzle pieces, when God began to reveal the mysteries. Homeschooling, my grandmother living with us, the gym, and all the love I felt from God connected us to His Kingdom, not the pattern of this world. Just as Christ stated in John 18:36, "My kingdom is not of this world." I wanted to live in this kingdom with God so I could experience peace of mind. It eventually came, but first I had to silence the voices of my will that wanted to remain in control. Deliverance from the darkness, that is, the resistance I heard from my flesh, was not only a works-based programmed process of reframing my thoughts, but it ultimately was a Holy Spirit overthrow!

In the hope that God would perform his word in my life, I meditated on the verse "Create in me a pure heart, O God, and renew a steadfast spirit within me," found in Psalm 51:10. Notice, this verse also had my birth numbers! When I was praying this verse, I spent a lot of time crying my eyes out to a dear friend from Classical Conversations during some of the biggest attacks in my marriage, mainly because I had the three issues taking up mental residence: sadness, anger, and fear. In a hopeless misunderstanding of us, Bobby and I made an agreement to divorce. I paid the attorney $1200 to start the process. Bobby did not expect that I would challenge him, but we were both exhausted in our relationship challenges. Things like pride, envy, lust, and gluttony will only make it more difficult to connect with your spouse and God. This creates division and isolation. The division is subtraction and separation. Jealousy and envy open doors to the enemy to attack your soul. Envy is probably the deadliest because it hides behind manipulation and control. Satan envied God's anointing and power, which showed up as a controlling spirit to gain power, kind of like a bully. When you surrender your power to a bully because you are afraid, this opens the door for many hidden evils to root inside yourself, such as anger. A bully wants you angry. Separation hurts, and anyone who has ever been hurt will try to comfort themselves through some kind of pleasure. When you are dividing, you can't multiply. Some would say fear is the opposite of love, which adds value, like multiplication. The world is like one big ball of math problems. It's abstract art!

I knew I had to let go of my own understanding and justification to be bitter about my relationship issues. After a long discussion as to the divide, I decided to trust God with my spiritual eyes, not by sight alone. I evicted the three tenants of sadness, anger, and fear. I remember going back to the attorney's office, sitting in the parking lot, praying, putting my covid mask of protection on and entering the building. I asked the Lord to allow me to get my money back if it was His will for us to stay together. I did get a refund except for the credit card fee. After this heart-shocking week in our marriage, we started a new journey to know ourselves better. The new journey to know myself better began after I was asked to part ways from the gym I had been connected with. As an act of redemption, Bobby helped me open C5 Fitness the year of our son's Senior year of high school. God opened a door for me to work for myself. My husband began to believe in us again. He started operating as he saw himself, with a new vision. He wanted freedom, too! My husband took an About Face, a 180-degree turnaround! I remember his fervent prayer to God in worship, whether I found him in the garage or the workout room, kneeling, crying, singing, or praying in the Spirit. I knew God was doing miraculous work in him. Although it took me a while to trust in us again, my husband was determined to fight for us. He had further struggles with his flesh (Don't we all!), but my forgiveness and love for him 70 x 7 opened the door for a double-blessing.

Love is greater than fear or any form of separation. It's important to remember to forget the attachment to earthly material or sensual pleasures. Instead, focus on some of the spiritual and abstract things like love, faithfulness, and compassion. Nurturing these qualities will help us grow our relationship with God which will overflow to others. Hebrews 11:6 declares, "Without faith, it is impossible to please God." I knew I could have faith that our relationship was meant to reflect love so that our children would know how to love well. Love is contagious, even though one can only see the evidence of this abstract intangible verb. Have you ever noticed how children light up with smiles when they see their parents loving each other with hugs and kisses? And, of course, the devil tries hard to create lies and illusions so this will not easily happen.

We have free will apart from God. The choice is yours. Free will is a powerful force, but it also comes with pain at times because of our humanness to be judgmental or unforgiving. It is important that we take personal ownership of our thoughts and choose for ourselves who we are because co-dependence is dangerous. You will struggle serving two masters: yourself and God. If I continued to depend upon affirmations and approval from my spouse rather than God, I was not a whole and confident woman. A close friend to our family prophesied, 'The devil knows that together, my husband and I would be very powerful if we stayed together, and that is why he wants to see us separate.' Her words penetrated our hearts and helped us to realize that our tensions were lessons for our success. Words have the potential to destroy or build, but it's more about the words you validate as truth. Perseverance builds character. Character is built through trials, and sometimes, your heart hurts through those trials. There were many years I had passion to serve him, but my heart hardened when I allowed my mind to ponder the disappointments. It's only by the miracle of God in my heart that my love for Bobby has renewed. I had to reframe my love for him as a soul to be nurtured. We all need love, so giving away what you need will help your needs to be met. Redemption that is heavenly is so much more beautiful and rewarding than any worldly redemption like that from a lottery ticket or exchange for goods. Neither of us will ever be perfect in our own eyes if we are looking through the lens of judgment and comparison. Bobby always claimed we are just two imperfect people trying our best to live in a fallen world.

Our self-worth is already established in Christ through his death, burial, and resurrection to those who believe; however, too many of us will still believe 'we have consequences for our choices.' So, by that statement, a person will live their life bound in shame and guilt and never be free to soar to their highest potential. Giving up an old identity or a world label may be the hardest mental work one has to do, but it's the only way to eternal joy and peace on earth. Christ said, 'My kingdom is not of this world.' We can experience heaven on earth within our mind since our minds does not know the difference between what is real and what is imaginary. I can imagine the fear, but nothing in real time has changed. If our human beliefs and understandings supersede our Maker's, then we may just miss the greatest blessing, the Kingdom of Heaven! That's what happened to Lucifer, and he was demoted! Stop and ask yourself, 'How big is God?' Do I know that his name, Immanuel, means God with us? Don't mistake yourself as a god, just tap into the spirit within you to imagine his possibilities and then do what he prompts in your heart. Our imaginations can grow, but God's imagination and power are always bigger.

I learned more about trusting Him as the source of peaceful confidence. I believe God was calling me to share my testimony in my mid-40s, and I needed to listen and obey! When I was a child, my dad would get so frustrated with me for not listening. 'Get the peanut butter out of your ears,' he'd call out. My mother and sister would yell, 'Listen!' when I would interrupt someone's story because I also had to comment about the topic. It took a long time to fully trust God, be patient, and watch the Lord reveal mysteries to me. There is an acronym for FROG (Fully Rely On God). We cannot find contentment and peace when we hop instead of stop. Being like a frog, we would pattern ourselves to hop from one thing to the next. Doing this, we may never authentically reflect our creator and unique design for His glory. So next time you feel like hopping, rest on the rock for a while. It took 25 years of marriage to finally break the Band-aid chain and find the grace and freedom of God for myself. If we don't do the heart work, we will continue to suffer with anxiety. Asking Jesus into your heart is like putting a new heart into your soul, and that new heart still needs to grow. It's like having an "open hand "on a new heart (the size of a fist) and instead of hopping like a rabbit be like a turtle and win the race! I believe we all have a desire to "break chains" and experience this freedom from oppression. Why would anyone want to suffer if there was a way not to suffer?

When we learn to listen and pay attention, we will understand the mysteries God is speaking at every moment to us. If you want your life to transform out of the darkness you may be experiencing, you must listen for the Holy Spirit's voice. We were friends with a couple when my son was about four years old. Years later, I saw their father in Walmart, and all he said to me was, 'Slow down.' No, he didn't even say 'hello or how are you? It's been a long time,' nope, he just said, 'Slow down!' God is still reminding me to slow down and, pay attention to the small things and be grateful for them! We must slow down, listen, and learn! Maybe the turtle mascot from my sorority modeled an idea that I was not aware of! Maybe God was saying, "Slow down!" If we skip this lesson of listening to the Spirit in this foundational stage, then we may end up understanding life through our own lenses, not God's lens as part of our story. At age 46, God sent me that message six times within one week! The scripture Psalm 46:10 says, "Be still and know that I am God." It's time to take the lid off ourselves, trust our Creator, and know that fear has no place in what God has planned for you. He is Lord of Lords and King of Kings. No other god can come before Him (this includes you). Let us lay aside our methods, lay aside our plans, and allow the Spirit of God to flow through his creation!

My daughter gave me a rose quartz heart necklace, and

mysteriously, I also received a gift from a family friend that was the same rock. It is said that this rock opens and heals the heart's energy center, where love is rooted.

The year 2022, *Redeeming Love* movie came out, and during Bobby's 47th year of life, I became certain that our hearts were together to tell a story, God's redeeming Love story! Years ago, I had to remove my wedding ring because it would break out and inflame my finger so that I could not get the ring on or off. After the movie, I was inspired to wear my ring again. It fit, and it did not break my skin out for a long time. I don't think this was any coincidence. Perspective does matter! It's almost like magic! Revival may be a term most people don't relate to. The prefix re- means to do it again. Vita means life in Latin. So, a revival is like having a new life or a great personal awakening. We are truly living a revival in our relationship, mostly because of our perspective shift, belief in love and forgiveness.

It's important that we write the calling and the vision God started in our hearts, because the story will have mysteries that could take you off track. God's timing is perfect and mysterious! The week following Easter 2022, The Lord brought my attention to John 20:22, "Receive the Holy Spirit."[24] At first, I did not think anything of it, but then I saw it! 2022! At my gym, I always share one word of the week and a scripture. Easter was on the 17th, and my breakthrough confirmation of what God would do came on the 30th. Just a little background, I'm a Taurus, and this was a big shift year

---

[24] John 20:21-22 NIV "Peace be with you! As the Father has sent me, I am sending you." And with that he breathed on them and said, "Receive the Holy Spirit."

for me, according to astrology. Big changes in significant times! In 2004, God confirmed my calling to homeschool. In 2012, a spiritual war started within our home and our country. In 2014, I started a new job at a Christian school. In 2019, I opened C5 Fitness, and in 2022, my gym went to a new spiritual level. The word of the week was "within." I've been doing a lot of personal growth lately, and this has helped me to search my heart and any limiting beliefs I have held based on my choices throughout my life. Ephesians 2:9 states, "Not by works, so that no one can boast." Zechariah 4:6 states, "Not by might nor by power, but by my Spirit." These two verses brought me back to the day I knew that I was supposed to homeschool, and at that point, I felt the holy spirit tell me, 'Everything is going to be ok!' Psalm 46:4-5 was part of a text I received from a friend that week, "There is a river whose streams make glad the city of God, the holy place where the Highest dwells. God is within her; she will not fall." This last verse was on a shirt that one of the first members of my gym gave to me. Also, before I started my gym there was a member of the old gym, where I coached, who gave me a tank top that had "Chain Breaker" on it. She did not know she was prophesying what God had been speaking to me all my life, and I could not see it because of all the Band-aids I was attached to! In 2022, I had two very vivid dreams, and I don't dream often. One was a room where water was pouring from the ceiling on the edges of the walls. I think this was prophesy of how hard my heart was but how God would let the water break if I could just forgive. The other dream, I was on a slide in the middle of the ocean. In this one, I was afraid. I thought maybe the slide represented a turning point. Remember, heart walls are not physical walls; and they are more like emotions and thoughts about yourself. I had a heart wall of hopelessness.

In 2022, I had a third dream, but this one was not a happy one. I was bleeding below the left knee but at the top of my calf. I wanted to cut my leg off because it hurt. This is what we do when we walk in the flesh and withhold love. We hurt! I knew I had to walk in the Spirit, surrender my own imagination and limitations, and trust that God would perfect the thing he started. I remember a sermon by a guest speaker at our church who spoke of throwing water over the people within the congregation. He said some will get wet, some will watch, and some will move. The Spirit of God will move you as you catch the wave of energy. Limitations are Band-aids, don't stick to them. Proverbs 23:7 scripture says, "As a man thinketh, so is he." If I focus on the thoughts that come by the patterns of this world, I would be stuck in the seat while watching others. Another powerful event happened. On the way home from the Unique program, I received a text from a lady in my Thursday bible study group. This was a picture of her grandmother's church notes. Immediately, I began to cry. The verse on it was Philippians 1:6, "being confident of this, that he who began a good work in you will carry it on to completion until the day of Christ Jesus." The Wednesday one week after Easter, I read my draft for my book to a friend. She said, "Stop, read that again!" I suppose the Spirit in her wanted to make sure my flesh heard what my Spirit had written in the draft. "Confidence comes from the Lord." When we turn back to the Lord, confidence returns too!

I've always trusted that God equips the called, anoints who he wants to, and places who he wants to in position. God wants to set the captives free, and I need to be set free! I'm so thankful that I was once bound, but now I am free! Breaking away from fear, worldly approval, and admiration, and just being who God created me to be. I love this kind of confidence!

The heart-to-heart ministry at our first church is so significant to me now because of my name and Bobby's name. My name means heart, and Bobby's last name means heart. We had several events that broke our hearts throughout our marriage, but God has redeemed every broken piece in my heart and his heart.

How do I know I hear from God? After the Unique weekend and the text messages, my 46th birthday came. My daughter asked me what I thought 46 meant. I had no reply, and it was just another birthday. The next day, I was taking a bath, and it hit me! Written on the wall was a cross with Psalm 46:10. How funny! I was 46 on the 10th of May! Well, for the next 10 days, God directed me to see this verse 5 times in different places! Two places in my own home, which I did not know was the same scripture. Then, on Wednesday evening as I was traveling to my client's house for a backyard movie night to watch Facing the Giants, I was listening to a song which I didn't know the title of. I searched the lyrics and found out the title was "Be Still." Then, the next morning, at my friend's house for bible study on Dr. Caroline Leaf's book "Switch on Your Brain" I was drinking coffee from a cup that had Psalm 46:10! I asked her if she had this cup last week, and she said the Lord told her to get more cups out for more ladies to join us and she said this one is for you. It's crazy that I did not notice the verse until my 2nd refill of coffee. For the 4th reminder, I was at a client's house to do her nutrition consultation, and I gazed up over her fireplace, and there the same picture at my house rested. That verse, Psalms 46:10! A couple of weeks later, tensions were high because of some unfortunate events, and the devil was trying to keep me from my friend's pool party. Well, I was able to make it there, and when I said the anointing was there, Yes, it was! There was a lady I met who gave me a bracelet she previously purchased without knowing why or who it was for. It had the same verse! She spoke a prophetic word over me and said that I would go into places and people would be set free because of the anointing of Jesus and that I would be the peace in the chaos. Wow! I was totally taken aback.

As evidence of God working in the stillness of my small gym, he allowed a gym group photo with those C5 wristbands to come up on my Facebook memories after two years of opening my C5 Fitness gym! I know that C5 Fitness is God's business, and he will get the glory for all his handiwork! As it says in Psalm 19: "The skies declare the work of his hands!" I have been learning how to become unattached from an expected outcome and not get weary in doing well. I've practiced breaking free from self-condemnation, all for God's glory!

I'm so glad I am no longer afraid of the world and the pleasures it offers the flesh, such as fame and fortune! No person or thing could ever satisfy what I have in Jesus! Just like a turtle in its shell, trusting if it is safe to extend its head, I believe that in Christ, though it is a hard life, we are safe in Him. He designed us to be hard and soft. We can be soft-hearted and stand firm like Mount Everest. We may have been beaten, humiliated, shamed, and rejected, but in Christ, we are raised with the same spirit so that we may experience life again and be free from any chains that have bound us. His crucifixion represented forgiveness and love for all mankind. Our lives are representations of Him. Everyone has pain, and some have more physical than emotional. Mine was emotional. I had to learn to let go of my pain story, embrace the fear, process it, overcome it, and free myself. It's time to get rid of the Band-aid and truly heal!

Perspective is position, position of mindset!

When I compared myself to anyone else, I lost my contentment to fear. It's not good to compare ourselves to others because that is when things begin to sink. That's what happened with Peter, the one Jesus called the 'Rock,' when he walked on water and then gave into his flesh, losing his focus on the Messiah. Remember, if you doubt, then you are going to do without the blessing for a time. Peace will come, but we don't get it without mastering it. Remember, to master anything, you must practice training the body that it is not to be the boss.

Relationships, external and within, can only heal with love. It's like blood! When you are bleeding, money can't help you. When you are dying, you need blood. I made an idol when I was younger. I religiously gave my blood to the Red Cross. If I missed my 56–60-day appointment, I panicked. God brought me to a place where I could close those doors. My iron dropped. This was for me, not against me. When iron no longer sharpens iron, it's time to start spending more time in the fire. The Redemption for "true" identity was coming! This blessing was so I could refocus on Him and know that I am a soul to be nurtured, not a product to be measured, nor a person tied to money or a label as a measuring weight, which is a heavy yoke.

I knew I really needed to focus on my gym and allow the

Spirit to bring me closer to the Lord. The year 2020, as many would describe it, was a mystery. After the country was shut down, including all tattoo shops, I randomly decided to get tattoos on each wrist: Love and forgive. Learning to let go, not just knowing I needed to let go, but applying the concept of letting go of my ego is true freedom. We will never be perfect enough in our separated states, and we must drive ourselves fervently forward to know the Father God who perfects that which he started. Love and Forgiveness conquered our past hurts.

The word "forgiveness" not only has religious and cultural implications, but it also embodies the idea that to be human is to exist in a way that isn't based on trade or commerce but rather on gifts. We were created to be gifts, not products or commodities, and forgiveness is a reminder of this. To forgive someone is to continue giving, even when it might be difficult. If we do not forgive, we cannot be forgiven. We always reap what we sow.

If we are created in God's image and likeness, we can only reflect the same gift-giving nature. If God is good, faithful, and always forgives, then it stands to reason that whatever we do, we cannot truly mess up God's plan. To recognize our imperfections, our sinfulness, and our need for forgiveness would then be to understand that we are called to forgive others.

Love is something that has inspired artists for centuries. It's a subject that has been written about extensively and one that still puzzles scientists. Falling in love alters our body chemistry, and scientists believe this is what causes the "love" or "butterflies in your stomach" feeling. Love also stimulates the part of our brain associated with pleasure. But as Christians, we believe that there's more to love than just good feelings. God is the source of love, and He is the embodiment of it. Jesus once said, hours before he was arrested, to his disciples that love would be the one identifying factor of his followers. *"By this all people will know that you are my disciples, if you have love for one another."* (John 13:35). In the Bible, 1 John mentions that 'God is love' and 'love comes from God'. Love has a deep and strong commitment that goes beyond feelings. Love protects, trusts, hopes, preserves, and never fails. That's what love is all about.

This newfound energy between Bobby and me started a chain-breaking reaction in my heart, and I began to love him again.

This scripture from 1 Corinthians 13:4-8 NIV is worth deep meditation:

> "Love is patient, love is kind. It does not envy, it does not boast, it is not proud. It does not dishonor others, it is not self-seeking, it is not easily angered, it keeps no record of wrongs. Love does not delight in evil but rejoices with the truth. It always protects, always trusts, always hopes, always perseveres. Love never fails."

I wish I could say that I never failed to give perfect love, but I did not know God's agape love as my identity until after age forty-six and the Redeeming Love experience from a change of heart. Perfect love casts out all fear.[25] God has

---

[25] I John 4:18

perfect love for us, even when we do not know Him well.

God created humans because he loves us and designed us to have a relationship with Him. Christians are supposed to believe that nothing can interfere with God's love for them. Love is supposed to be constant and everlasting, never depending on our actions. The problem is that though we claim to believe in love like this, we don't live like there is evidence of that faith. Being a Christian or a Baptist (or any religion that one believes in) means nothing if one doesn't have love and if Christ was not raised from the dead. Love is something that we all have inside of us. Love is the foundation, but we often do not come to Jesus as our foundation. If you put Love in a picture frame with the border of unforgiveness, meaning you can't love because you can't forgive, then this creates an image that there are boundaries to love. I believe the borders of love through a human's eye are unbelief and fear of forgiving those we think need punishment. It's said that anger is the opposite of love, but that's not entirely accurate. Anger is the denial of love's existence in our lives. We've all felt anger and rage before because we can't seem to forgive someone or unburden ourselves from past emotions that are holding us back and tying us to negative memories. Forgiveness is key to moving on and growing as a person. I believe this is the act of removing the frame or the border.

If we want to achieve harmonious relationships, it's important that we learn to forgive and forget the negative experiences from our past life. Whether it's an ex, a boss, or even a family member, holding onto grudges and resentments will only block us from having healthy and fulfilling relationships. So, take some time to forgive yourself and others, and you'll start to see more harmony flow into every area of your life and in every relationship you establish. I've had to ask God to forgive me for holding a grudge against Him! Sometimes, we get angry with God, and then we must come back to repentance in order to restore a healthy relationship with Him. There is nothing wrong with confession of wrongdoings or wayward thoughts, just don't stay in a worthlessness mindset about yourself. Ricardo Sanchez wrote a song called "Moving Forward", which stuck with me and gave me the courage to let go of unforgiveness and move forward with a new and fresh anointing. This restores inner peace. It helps if you confess with your mouth out loud and say, "I forgive myself (or _____) for _____, and I receive peace and acceptance for the good that will follow this lesson."

As followers of Christ, we are called to extend grace and forgiveness to others, just as God has forgiven us. Jesus not only calls us to forgive those who have wronged us but also to love them. *"You shall love your neighbor as yourself."* (Matt. 22:38 NASB).

True forgiveness can be a powerful tool for overcoming the past and moving on from suffering. It can renew relationships and allow for new opportunities for reconciliation and restoration with those who we have wronged. If we can learn to forgive, we can free ourselves to live a life of love, truth, and justice.

If you want to accelerate and deepen your spiritual growth, the single most effective way to do so is to reflect on how Scripture applies to your life. This reflection is more than just skimming a morning devotional or scanning your Bible before bed. It requires you to think carefully and critically about the things that inspire you so that you can understand them more fully.

Reflection is a process that we can all engage in to make sense of our experiences, both good and bad. By reflecting on our past, we can gain a new understanding and appreciation of our present situation. This can be beneficial both for individuals and for groups, as it can help us to see things from different perspectives and deepen our understanding.

A righteous person is one who believes and follows the faith-filled way that leads to life. They live like Christ, the way of love and forgiveness. So, righteousness is the practice of faith and work, living morally and virtuously. As we are being sanctified, we are filled with the righteousness of God. Our faith makes us whole. This is a big blessing because it means we can be more like Him. When you see your sins no more, you understand what love means. Jesus' blood covered our sins and kept no record of wrongs. Our faith declared us righteous, not by man's eyes but by His goodness and His ability to do in us what we could not do on our own. We could never perform enough right things to be declared righteous by our works or by-laws. All of us have broken the 10 commandments! We are weak in our flesh, but his Way (the Spirit) is strong. We have His strength living through our human weakness.

One of the best things about living in God's righteousness is that it's free - but it came at a high cost to Jesus. The price of righteousness is so high that no amount of money in the world could ever buy it. But that's the point! He is the Redeemer! God doesn't require us to purchase something we could never afford. It has already been paid in full through his own death to himself!

As you follow the path of Jesus, you see many changes coming into your life. Shame will lift off of you because you will feel loved and accepted. This releases the power of sin as the governing authority over your life. You may feel like you've been given a new identity and literally feel like you've been washed. You may experience new loving relationships or redemption with whole Spirit-filled people. Often, through this redemption process, you may be more understanding and less critical of others. Your responses may surprise you.

The Way of Jesus will guide you if you listen and learn from his eternal Spirit. He will meet you in your darkest hour, evolve your life to a better end and make sure you stay enlightened. Get out of your grave clothes, out of the cave, help others around you, do your part to make the world a better place, and live limitlessly. Opportunities are always coming into your life. Don't get so caught up in your own little world that you forget about the One who created you and wants to have a relationship with you.

To strengthen your relationship with God and develop a strong faith, love God with all your heart, soul, and mind. *"Teacher, which is the great commandment in the Law?" And he said to him, "You shall love the Lord your God with all your heart and with all your soul and with all your mind. This is the great and first commandment."* (Matthew 22:36-38 ESV)

To know God and make Him known, I believe is to know yourself and others through life experiences. You cannot have a strong relationship with someone unless you take the time to get to know them. To know God means you know "true" love! Love keeps no record of wrongs (sin). When you invite the Holy Spirit into your life, you experience God! You will be broken, you will be free, and you will become the image of somebody everyone needs. Your reflection will not be who you are but who He is. You will be One! ONE FLESH! Oh, how beautiful is Oneness!

Because we live in a sin-natured world, don't become discouraged if you are not perfect enough, just keep moving forward in faith. I have never seen anyone's life progressively, linearly, and steadfastly improve because life is like the moon, waxing and waning. The problem is that we identify with the waning part, the losing a part of the whole, instead of the process of both. The song by Casting Crowns *Slow Fade,* will teach you that it's important to be careful what you do and say because someone is watching. You won't be perfect, but your quick return to the Lord will feel so much better. Don't stay in the waning. Maturity is embracing the highs and the lows without attachment to the emotion in what was lost or gained. Like people who diet, always struggling to keep the weight from returning, remembering these trials and victories may be waxing and waning. We never achieve perfection until we die of these visions and vain imaginations. Daily, we may fall into what is common, but a Champion keeps getting back up. Although COVID-19 shut down the gyms, I kept going with my vision and desire to help people have a healthy spirit, mind, and body. If the spirit of one's mission is lost, then the mind and body go downhill fast. I promoted change from the normal propaganda in gyms and across Hollywood to a more spiritual, intuitive focus. The objective for the C5 Fitness gym in 2020 was to create healthy lifestyles by breaking away from toxic cycles and mental strongholds or obsessions such as control. The more we measure, compare, and analyze, then the more our spirits hurt. We are souls to be nurtured, not products to be measured or controlled. It's one thing to grow in knowledge, it's another thing to lose your spirit. It has taken me many years to learn, but by the grace of God and a mustard seed of faith, I'm awakening to truth! My greatest challenge became my mission: to love and forgive. I needed to love and forgive myself and others to truly walk with God and experience peace within. As Terry La Masters quoted, "Your greatest victory is on the other side of your greatest struggle."

Forgiveness became my function in 2023. I recognized that my parents, my spouse, and my tough experiences were teaching me how to love myself, love God, and trust God's plan, so I must be thankful. They were perfect in God's eyes, and that's when I began to see my own "true identity!" If I was judging them, I was not seeing clearly. To become your unique self, I believe you must learn through heart transformation. For some this work of redemption takes years of repeat cycles. Heart transformation work has five steps: ownership, discipline, choices, consequences, and lastly freedom comes in like "a new birth." We receive because we believe, we doubt and do without, and then finally, we mount up with wings like an eagle! Some say or imagine this like a butterfly. Transformation!

The mysteries of my life could have bound me, but they freed me! Think about what it feels like to be caged or boxed in, and then think about what it feels like to live free! Maya Angelou's book, "I Know Why the Caged Bird Sings," became a key to unlocking my freedom. The quote, "A caged bird sings of freedom, a free bird flies," literally changed my desire to live without limits.

Chapter Five

Grace

My life lessons have been molded and shaped because of great parents and life challenges. I give a lot of grace to my parents because I truly believe they love me. It's easier to forgive them now that I am an adult, probably because I am also a mother. When we believe things are against us, we only see fear, and we learn to self-protect. I found God's grace is sufficient in mysterious ways, like a puzzle with a missing piece. Until we make peace with God, we may not see the big picture. He reveals things when we heal spiritually within Him. I could not understand the long-suffering of my marriage, which almost ended in 2020 when COVID made us all socially crazy. Don't get me wrong, there are wonderful moments in my marriage and that is why we are still together! There is something about five and twenty-five! Grace upon grace! There is a mysterious beauty in numbers and words.

Like many of us in need of God's grace, my dad received grace. See John 1:16 NIV, "Out of his fullness, we have all received grace in place of grace already given." Interestingly, that verse about grace found in John 1:16 happens to be my father's birthday! He is a man who has received much grace! He is a miracle! This awakening to this verse confirmed in my heart that my dad's grace would be passed down to me. In 2022, he could have lost his life in a gas fire. God's grace poured out and saved his life.

For many years, maybe the last five years, my daughter and I have seen the number 47, which was a transformational age for my husband. The number four represents man's weakness. The number seven means complete. We saw 47 on many clocks, prices of items, and mailboxes for people who were also part of our story. I asked a friend about this number, and she said it may mean completing a test. The Israelites were in the wilderness for 40 years. I do feel that I have had many spiritual tests which God has graciously allowed me to retake until I learned to trust him! Just like my gym, C5 Fitness, aka "C5 Life" gym, I believe I learned the meaning of Proverbs 3:5-6, "Trust in the Lord with all your heart and lean not on your own understanding." Grace and the story of overcoming the flesh is within each of us as we experience the pains and pleasures of this world. Jesus endured the cross and publicly exposed himself in order to set us free! Titus 2:11 states, "God's readiness to give and forgive is now public. Salvation's available for everyone!"[26]

The goodness of God is Grace! It is a gift from God that should fill us with thankfulness. There is no other gift more precious than the grace of God, as the Message Bible in Hebrews 2:9 says, "By God's grace, he fully experienced death in every person's place." I'm very thankful for this free gift, which was the key to my perspective shift that led to my freedom in Christ! It is written in Ephesians 2:8-9 NIV, *"For it is by grace you have been saved, through faith—and this is not from yourselves, it is the gift of God—not by works, so that no one can boast."*

If our motives are not in alignment with our desire to please God, we will not thrive because we will be vainly surviving in our striving against the enemy. I believe I was pre-destined to become a homeschool mom, a gym coach, and a believer in

---

[26] Titus 2:11 NIV

Jesus. I learned so much about God through trials and tribulations. Though my journey involved a lot of confusion and change, it was imperative that I discover the spiritual foundation I had rejected.[27]

Everyone has been given the opportunity to know this freedom, but some will continue to live in bondage and fear. Some will still think we don't deserve the blessings because we have not earned it, or some may see God differently. When I took the time to record some of my life mysteries, I began to understand how God used my mess to make something beautiful. Once you ask, the door will be open to you, and you will see the signs and wonders, and then you'll begin to understand that if it wasn't for God's grace, you'd have to be your own hero. God is not the villain some make him out to be. I honestly feel that we are our own villain until we become our own hero through our surrender and obedience to God. Sometimes we worship the wrong thing, we hope in the wrong things, and we attract the wrong things, but His grace is sufficient. We should not neglect the work within us! In Matt 20:16, Jesus stated, *"So the last shall be first, and the first last: for many be called, but few chosen."*

If we allow wild discovery, like a child, God our Father in Heaven will draw us to him. Children gravitate toward love. I thought I had messed up my life, I thought there was no redemption, I thought God wasn't helping me, and all along His grace was drawing me in. It is by His loving grace that now I am free! I am not condemned, punished, or suffering. A broken heart is mended with love and forgiveness. Maybe those tattoos on my wrist were part of the whole tapestry! After 2020, it all

---

[27] Mark 12:10-11

started to make sense. It was like destiny found me. My daughter shared a book with me called A Course in Miracles. I started a new mindset with this teaching, and it helped me unlock the ability to love without conditions. It can never replace the Bible, but I learned to think deeper from this text. I took ownership of my perspective and found it a lot easier to forgive and love rather than harbor bitterness about drastic changes because the change was "for" me, not against me. Forgiving and loving myself was harder than offering it to others.

Bitterness is linked with brittle bones and cancer. Ouch! A person with heart walls is suffering. It's like a dam with lots of water pressure! It would be a disaster if the dam wall broke, so we avoid helping hurt people. I'd rather be lost in an ocean! It's fun to ride the waves without restriction, resistance, or fear. But many of us are afraid to cry or show weakness, especially if you are in leadership. Think about a pregnant woman about to give birth; the pressure is so intense, but let the water break, and the baby will be delivered. The pressure of feeling like you are dying, and then you release the child to the world, and you relax, knowing that the pain has ceased for a bit.

When I became just a nobody for the sake of dying to my flesh, I witnessed limitless possibilities. NO MORE BAND-AIDS! I was free to live by the Spirit, letting go of all vanity and learning to "be still." In 2024, I had a turtle tattooed on my left bicep with the scripture Psalm 46:10 "Be still, and know…" That reminder helped me heal from all my busy-brained fears that God forgot about me.

When life throws you lemons, make lemonade out of the lemons. I know it is hard because the six-inch battle between our ears may feel overwhelming. We strive too hard! Surrender your will to the Lord. We give up on God too quickly! Surviving is not the goal, thriving is. So many of us play the role of victim when we could be victors! My hope for our nation is to unite through diversity, like my sorority, and respectfully commerce with transparency, like a torn veil. Many people are starving for approval, admiration, attention, and acceptance, while hiding the authenticity which God created! The world of people could improve if we kept the Golden Rule toward ourselves and others. Love yourself and others in a healthy way. Slowing down and breathing will help you gain clarity. Observing many life lessons which I have experienced in my homeschooling days, my marriage, and work opportunities, helped me gain wholeness because I did the hardest thing, the heart work. When we unite our heart, soul, and mind back to the Father, our Creator, we become limitless!

I have this cross-image in my mind. Our head, our heart, and our gut are the vertical alignments we struggle with, and the horizontal is the message we send to others. The space between our head and heart is a shorter distance. We can have knowledge that comes out of our mouth, but when that knowledge gets to our heart, our passion flows to others. But when the knowledge just goes to the brain and out the mouth it might as well be vomit. It is said that our gut and brain are alike. What we put into our mouth affects our brain and gut. Jesus said, in Matthew 15:11 "What goes into someone's mouth does not defile them, but what comes out of their mouth, that is what defiles them." We know our words are important, but we misuse them. It's at that crossroads, our heart, where we get stuck. We can either be old and broken, or we can be new and well.

I believe God's grace is a big part of my identity and

freedom. Not only is my favorite number five, probably because my nickname was "Number 5!" but my gym model is built around it too; It's the C5 Life: A Commission of Grace. I had no idea then that this number Five would hold such significance in my life. It wasn't until I was an adult that I learned that the fifth letter (H) of the Hebrew alphabet, pronounced Hei, meant Grace.

Throughout the Bible, we read about imperfect people who failed to keep the law but were provided grace, nonetheless. Abram failed to trust and obey God, when he started a new lineage with Hagar, but God's grace was with him. He still became the father of many nations. His name was changed to Abraham! "No longer shall your name be called Abram, but your name shall be Abraham, for I made you a father of many nations." [28] The letter H was added to Abraham's name and Sarah's name after they became members of God's family. This wasn't done through circumcision but instead through faith. The five great mysteries have always been the Father, Son, Holy Spirit, Creation, and Redemption. Because the creation was cursed, or made weak, it started to worship vanity itself. We tried to earn God's grace through religion and works, which is dead. As the scripture says in Proverbs 14:12, "There is a way that appears to be right, but in the end, it leads to death." There is no way I could have saved myself from the two car accidents, so God's hand moved the chess piece in my favor. His grace also spared me from giving up my own life or divorcing my wonderful husband! God blessed me with the opportunity to know Him through several influential people! Each day is a gift, learn to treasure yourself and your uniqueness which God put

---

[28] Genesis 17:5

within you and all the other people in your world around you. Remember, God is the author. He writes the script for us all! He gets all the credit for turning the impossible into possible, we get to reveal all the good news. He is the invincible invisible cover label, and we get to hide within Him, though we can only see evidence of his presence.

We never know what legacy we leave behind. Moses may not have entered the Promised Land, but he was a key leader! He didn't even believe in himself because of his stuttering problem. Moses was the leader of the Israelites, and they constantly complained. This kept them in the wilderness for 40 years. If he really understood the power of his words as if they were like swords, then he could have possibly saved many years. If you read the account of the Israelites in Exodus 17, God told Moses to speak to the rock, but he jumped ahead of God and did not listen and he struck the rock. Then the Israelites were able to get water from the rock. The hard rock miraculously split, like the curtain when Jesus took his last breath on the cross! I believe this is symbolic of the Holy Spirit, a gift we did not earn. Jesus is the water of life; he keeps us alive by his grace! Another story in the bible that resonates with my passion about the number five is the story of David and Goliath. David did not want Saul's heavy armor and he went to battle practically naked with the giant and his five smooth stones. It only took One Rock to overcome the giant. He had a heart after God because he trusted the One and Only!

To live as the least of these, like a child, reflects innocence. When Jesus told the Sermon on the Mount, he taught us to see, but all we did was listen and repeat it over and over. Scripture states in Mark 10:15, *"Truly I tell you, anyone, who will not receive the kingdom of God like a little child will never enter it."* It took me a long time to receive the Kingdom of Heaven on earth. Suffering was not pleasant, but it did help transform me from the inside out. I did not understand what it meant to be in God's will. I was rebellious and mentally lost; therefore, I was in the will of myself, not God. God's will and your will united are like salt and pepper, they go together, they bring order and understanding. It's like we are in darkness, until we come to the light. When we rest in his will, everything will work together for our good.

In the Fall of 2022, I teamed up with Revelation Wellness ®. We were challenged to pray and seek a word that we felt the Lord put into our hearts. I wrote the word on my left bicep: Create. We all have different words that speak to us, but I know this for myself, God created in me a voice. The devil may have tried to take it away in 2019, just before I left my previous gym, but my voice stood on the rock of my salvation because I decided not make any agreement to stay captive to fear. Trusting in the Lord with all your heart, creating a wonderful life, full of love and forgiveness, is freedom! May the butterfly fly! May the band-aid be pulled off! May the heart, beat again! God did the work within me! He said, "It is finished!"[29] With that, we receive the greatest gift, his Spirit! I Corinthians 15:10, "But by the grace of God I am what I am, and his grace to me was not without effect. No, I worked harder than all of them—yet not I, but the grace of God that was with me." Interestingly, the last trail I hiked was Panther Creek and at the end of our trail I picked up a random iron fork! When we die to ourselves, we can truly say, "The best is yet to come!"

---

[29] John 19:30 NIV

www.ingramcontent.com/pod-product-compliance
Lightning Source LLC
Chambersburg PA
CBHW052143070526
44585CB00017B/1955